# 75 FLORAL BLOCKS TO CROCHET

# 75 FLORAL BLOCKS TO CROCHET

Beautiful Patterns to Mix and Match for
Afghans, Throws, Baby Blankets, and More

## BETTY BARNDEN

St. Martin's Griffin
New York

75 FLORAL BLOCKS TO CROCHET
Copyright © 2012 Quarto, Inc. All rights reserved.
Printed in China. For information, address St. Martin's Press,
175 Fifth Avenue, New York, N.Y. 10010.

www.stmartins.com

Library of Congress Cataloging-in-Publication Data Available
Upon Request

ISBN: 978-1-250-01332-3

First U.S. Edition: September 2012

10 9 8 7 6 5 4 3 2 1

Conceived, designed, and produced by
Quarto Publishing plc
The Old Brewery
6 Blundell Street
London N7 9BH

QUAR: HKC

**Project Editor:** Victoria Lyle
**Art Editor and Designer:** Julie Francis
**Pattern Checker:** Lucille Kazel
**Illustrator (charts):** John Woodcock, Kuo Kang Chen
**Illustrator (techniques):** Kuo Kang Chen
**Photographer (directory and technical section):** Philip Wilkins
**Photographer (projects):** Nickey Dowey
**Indexer:** Helen Snaith
**Art Director:** Caroline Guest

**Creative Director:** Moira Clinch
**Publisher:** Paul Carslake

Color separation by Pica Digital Pte Ltd, Singapore
Printed by 1010 Printing International Ltd, China

# CONTENTS

Foreword/About this book     6

## 1 USEFUL TECHNIQUES

Materials and equipment     10

Yarn and block sizes     12

Abbreviations and symbols     14

Directions of working     16

Block arrangements     18

Joining blocks     20

Edgings     22

Planning a project     26

## 2 DIRECTORY OF BLOCKS

| | |
|---|---|
| Spring green | 32 |
| Sky blue | 38 |
| Summer pink | 42 |
| Harvest gold | 48 |

## 3 INSTRUCTIONS

| | |
|---|---|
| Triangles | 54 |
| Squares | 67 |
| Diamonds | 93 |
| Hexagons | 99 |
| Circles | 119 |

## 4 PROJECTS

| | |
|---|---|
| Busy Lizzie throw | 134 |
| Flower purses | 136 |
| Daisy cushion | 138 |
| Rose scarf | 140 |
| Index | 142 |
| Resources and credits | 144 |

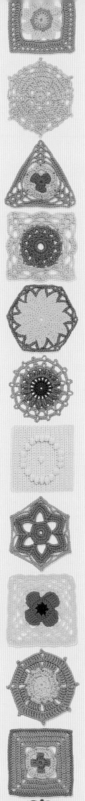

# FOREWORD

All the crochet blocks in this book are based on flowers, although some are more realistic than others.

Some blocks are adapted from traditional crochet designs, and use familiar techniques. In general, these are more abstract, less realistic. Many are quite simple to work, and use only one or two colors. Try working them in different color combinations, chosen to suit the purpose you have in mind.

On the other hand, most of the more complicated blocks have been especially designed for this book. These attempt to express the colors and shapes of particular flowers, using combinations of different stitches and unusual constructions to form the different flower parts. As a rule, the flower color(s) will be dictated, more or less, by the featured flower, but the background colors can be varied in any way you choose.

As a keen gardener, I love watching the seasons and the different flowers they bring, so I relished the challenge of choosing and designing the blocks for this book. In the garden, my favorite flower is always the one due to bloom in a week or two; when working on this book, my favorite block was always the one I had in mind to make next!

**BETTY BARNDEN**

# ABOUT THIS BOOK

This book provides a delightful collection of over 75 floral blocks to crochet. Each is both charming in its own right and looks fantastic when worked with others to create throws, cushions, scarves, or other projects of your own devising.

### CHAPTER 1: USEFUL TECHNIQUES (pages 8–29)

As well as covering basics such as equipment, yarn, abbreviations, and symbols, this chapter also contains techniques for using the blocks in this book, such as block arrangement, joining blocks, edgings, and planning a project.

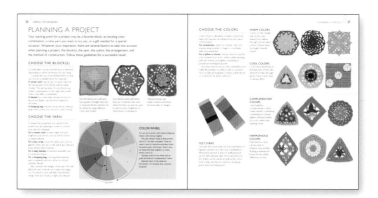

## SIZE

Blocks of the same shape are all the same size, for easy mixing and matching. All of the blocks in the Directory were worked using double knitting (DK) weight yarn and size E (3.5 mm) hook. They measure as follows:

Triangle: 6 in (15 cm)
Square: 5½ in (14 cm)
Diamond: 5½ x 7 in (14 x 18 cm)
Hexagon: 5 in (13 cm)
Circle: 5½ in (14 cm)

For more on yarns and block sizes, see pages 12–13.

## CHAPTER 2: DIRECTORY OF BLOCKS (pages 30–51)

The Directory is a showcase of the over 75 beautiful designs featured in this book. Organized into four color themes—spring green, sky blue, summer pink, harvest gold—it contains a mix of shapes and skill levels. Flick through this colorful visual guide, select your design, and then turn to the relevant page of instructions to create your chosen piece.

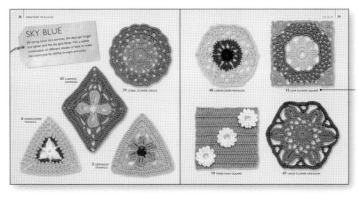

Each block is labeled with a number that corresponds to the relevant pattern in the Instructions chapter.

The skill level and method of working are indicated.

The colors used are indicated.

## CHAPTER 3: INSTRUCTIONS (pages 52–131)

In this chapter you'll find a written pattern and a chart for every design. The blocks are organized by shape to enable easy mixing and matching, as all the blocks of the same shape are the same size.

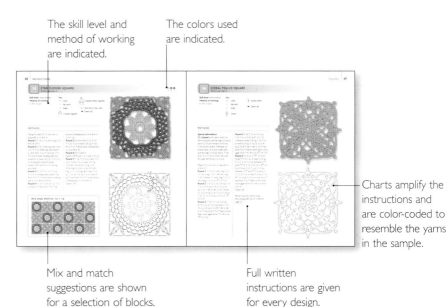

Charts amplify the instructions and are color-coded to resemble the yarns in the sample.

Mix and match suggestions are shown for a selection of blocks.

Full written instructions are given for every design.

## CHAPTER 4: PROJECTS (pages 132–141)

The blocks in this book can be combined and used in a myriad of ways. This chapter presents a selection of stunning designs to inspire you with ideas of how to use the blocks in your own projects.

Each project is illustrated with a photograph of the finished item.

# 1
## USEFUL TECHNIQUES

As well as covering basics such as equipment, yarn, abbreviations, and symbols, this chapter also contains techniques for using the blocks in this book, such as block arrangement, joining blocks, edgings, and planning a project.

# MATERIALS AND EQUIPMENT

The basic tools for crochet are simple, portable, and relatively inexpensive.

## HOOKS

Crochet hooks are the most important tools in your collection. Good quality crochet hooks are smooth and free of snags, and feel comfortable in your hand.

Crochet hooks are available in a range of materials, such as aluminum, bamboo, plastic, and resin. Aluminum hooks work well with woolly and fuzzy yarns, whereas bamboo hooks can help to control smooth, slippery yarns. Sometimes changing from, say, a plastic hook to a bamboo hook can affect the size of your finished block; always check your gauge carefully (page 12). Hooks are also made in different styles, such as with a flattened thumb rest, or (for small metal hooks) a wider wooden or plastic handle. Try out the different styles to see which suits you best.

As a rule, the finer the yarn, the smaller the suitable hook. The size of hook you use, together with the type of yarn chosen, will affect the finished size of the blocks you make (see pages 12–13).

### USEFUL TIP

Where a yarn label gives a recommended metric knitting needle size, a crochet hook of a similar metric size will usually give a satisfactory result.

This table shows both the American system of hook sizing and the international metric system, although the two systems do not correspond exactly. Even smaller hooks are available for very fine crochet threads.

## WHICH HOOK SIZE?

| Suitable for these yarns | U.S. steel hooks | U.S. plastic or aluminum hooks | Metric sizes (approx.) |
|---|---|---|---|
| 2-ply, light fingering | 6<br>5<br>4 | | 1.75 mm |
| 3-ply, fingering | 3<br>2<br>1<br>0 | B | 2 mm<br>2.25 mm<br>2.5 mm |
| 4-ply, fingering, sock | 00 | C<br>D | 2.75 mm<br>3 mm |
| sport, double knitting (DK), light worsted | | E<br>F<br>G | 3.5 mm<br>4 mm |
| worsted, aran | | H<br>I | 4.5 mm<br>5 mm<br>5.5 mm |
| chunky, bulky | | J<br>K | 6 mm<br>6.5 mm<br>7 mm |
| super chunky, super bulky | | L<br>M<br>N | 8 mm<br>9 mm<br>10 mm |

1.75 mm

B/2.25 mm

C/2.75 mm

G/4 mm

H/5 mm

K/6.5 mm

M/9 mm

## ACCESSORIES

It is useful to keep a few other items in your work bag.

### YARN NEEDLES

These are used for sewing seams and for darning in yarn tails (1). Yarn needles have blunt tips, to avoid splitting stitches. They are available in different sizes. Choose a yarn needle to suit the weight of your yarn. The eye should be large enough to easily take the yarn you are using.

### PINS

Glass-headed pins (2) have large heads, and are the best type to use for blocking (page 20). Safety pins are useful when joining blocks together, to enable you to match the stitches and corners exactly.

### SCISSORS

Use a pair of small, sharp scissors to cut yarn cleanly (3).

### RULER AND TAPE MEASURE

A small ruler is best for checking the size of your blocks to obtain the gauge you want (see page 12). A tape measure is useful for larger measurements (4).

### STITCH MARKERS

Use this type of split marker (5) to hold the working loop when you put your work aside, or when you leave a color aside that you will later return to. Markers can also be used as an aid to counting, for example when working a long edging.

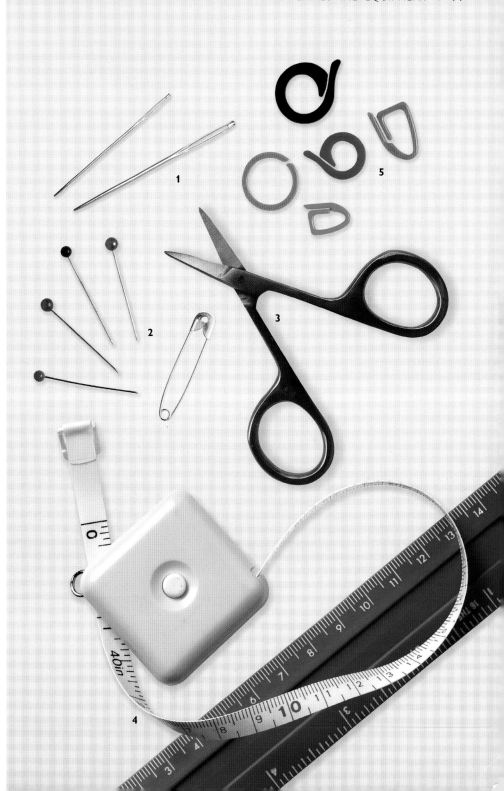

*The swatches above show the blocks at real size and demonstrate how yarn and hook size can dramatically change the appearance and feel of the same design.*

# YARNS AND BLOCK SIZES

The weight of yarn you choose (together with the hook size) will dictate the finished size of the block you make.

The Off-center square (block 37, page 90) is shown here made in six different weights of yarn, each worked with the corresponding suitable size of hook (see table on page 10).

It is possible to change the size of a block slightly, by using a hook one or two sizes smaller or larger than recommended. However, this will affect the feel of the finished block; using a smaller hook makes a firmer block (which may be fine for a purse, perhaps, but unsuitable for a shawl), while using a larger hook will make a looser block, which may not keep its shape in use.

3 in (7.5 cm) square

4¼ in (11 cm) square

5 in (12.5 cm) square

5½ in (14 cm) square

*2-ply cotton yarn worked with a US size 5 hook (approx. 1.75 mm).*

*4-ply cotton yarn worked with a US size 1 hook (approx. 2.5 mm).*

*Sport weight wool worked with a US size E hook (approx. 3.5 mm).*

*Double knitting weight silk/wool blend worked with a US size G hook (approx. 4 mm).*

## TO TEST YOUR GAUGE

Always test your own gauge before starting any project.

1 Make a block with the yarn you want to use and a suitable hook (see table on page 10) and press or block the work (see page 20).
2 Measure the block across the center with a small ruler (for a triangular block, measure the length of the sides).
3 If your block is too small, try again with a larger hook. If your block is too large, make another with a smaller hook.

6½ in (16.5 cm) square

7 in (18 cm) square

*Aran wool worked with a US size H hook (approx. 5 mm).*

*Bulky alpaca/cotton yarn worked with a US size J hook (approx. 6 mm).*

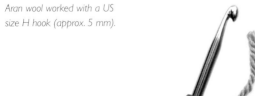

# ABBREVIATIONS AND SYMBOLS

There is no worldwide standard for crochet abbreviations and symbols, but below is a list of those used in this book.

## ABBREVIATIONS AND SYMBOLS

Abbreviations and symbols may vary from one pattern publisher to another, so always check that you understand the system in use before commencing work.

| Stitch or term | Abbreviation | Symbol |
|---|---|---|
| chain | ch | o |
| slip stitch | ss | • |
| single crochet | sc | + |
| half double | hdc | |
| double | dc | |
| treble | tr | |
| double treble | dtr | |
| bobble | B |  e.g. bobble of 5 doubles |
| puff stitch | PS | e.g. puff of 4 half doubles |
| popcorn | PC | e.g. popcorn of 5 doubles |
| back loop | bl | e.g. single in back loop |
| front loop | fl | e.g. half double in front loop |
| chain space | ch sp | (none) |
| together | tog | (none) |
| yarn round hook | yrh | (none) |
| group | gp | (none) |
| pattern | patt | (none) |
| beginning | beg | (none) |
| following | foll | (none) |
| alternate | alt | (none) |
| remaining | rem | (none) |
| repeat | rep | (none) |

Some patterns include special abbreviations, which are explained on the instructions pages.

## ARRANGEMENTS OF SYMBOLS

### SYMBOLS JOINED AT TOP
A group of symbols may be joined at the top, indicating that these stitches should be worked together at the top.

### SYMBOLS JOINED AT BASE
Symbols joined at the base should all be worked into the same stitch below.

Puff    Bobble    Popcorn

### SYMBOLS JOINED AT TOP AND BASE
Sometimes a group of stitches are joined at both top and bottom, making a puff, bobble, or popcorn.

### SYMBOLS ON A CURVE
Sometimes symbols are drawn at an angle, depending on the construction of the stitch pattern.

### DISTORTED SYMBOLS
Some symbols may be lengthened, curved, or spiked, to indicate where the hook is inserted below.

# READING CHARTS

Each design in this book is accompanied by a chart, which should be read together with the written instructions. The chart represents the right side of the work.

## CHARTS IN ROWS

*Right side rows are numbered at the right, and read from right to left.*

*Wrong side rows are numbered at the left, and read from left to right.*

*Rows are numbered, beginning row 1 (which may be at bottom right or bottom left, as here).*

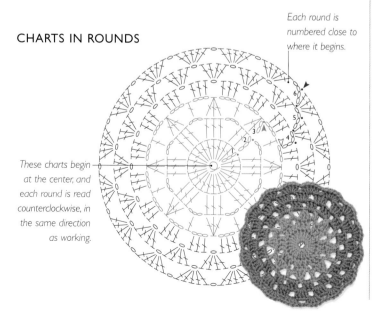

## CHARTS IN ROUNDS

*Each round is numbered close to where it begins.*

*These charts begin at the center, and each round is read counterclockwise, in the same direction as working.*

# BALL BANDS

Most yarns have a paper band or tag attached with vital information such as the weight of the ball or skein, fiber composition, yardage, and how to look after your finished item. The band may also recommend hook and knitting needle sizes and give gauge details.

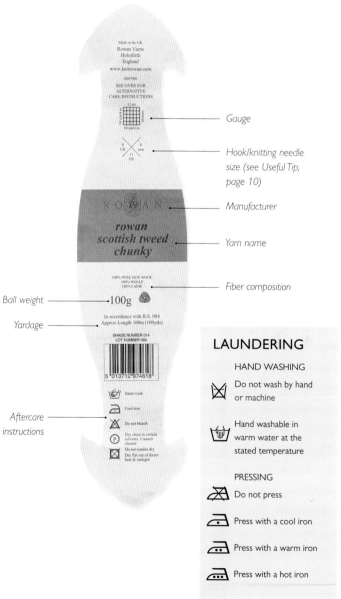

Gauge

Hook/knitting needle size (see *Useful Tip, page 10*)

Manufacturer

Yarn name

Fiber composition

Ball weight

Yardage

Aftercare instructions

## LAUNDERING

### HAND WASHING

Do not wash by hand or machine

Hand washable in warm water at the stated temperature

### PRESSING

Do not press

Press with a cool iron

Press with a warm iron

Press with a hot iron

# DIRECTIONS OF WORKING

Crochet can be worked in rows or in rounds. The method of working for each block in this book is indicated in the instructions.

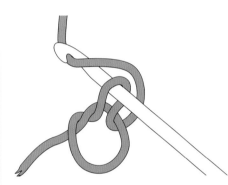

## ROWS OR ROUNDS

Blocks worked in rows are worked back and forth. As a rule, each row begins with a number of turning chains, which count as the first stitch of the row: 1 ch = 1 sc, 2 ch = 1 hdc, 3 ch = 1 dc, and so on. On the following row, the last stitch is worked into the top of the turning chains.

Blocks worked in the round are worked outward from the center in a counterclockwise direction. Each round normally begins with a number of starting chains (the equivalent of the turning chains used when working in rows), and each round closes with a slip stitch worked into the top of these chains. The starting chain(s) at the beginning of a round, together with the slip stitch at the end, are counted as the first stitch of the round.

Some blocks are worked in both rows and rounds, for example the Dandelion diamond (block 40, page 93), which consists of a central panel worked in rows, with an outer border worked in rounds.

Some blocks begin with the length of two edges, and stitches are decreased at the center on every row, ending at the top corner.

## WORKING IN THE ROUND

Blocks worked in the round begin at the center with either a fingerwrap or a ring of chains.

### FINGERWRAP
This method closes the center tightly, leaving no hole unless a large number of stitches are worked on the first round.

Sometimes called a slip ring, a fingerwrap is made by winding the yarn once or twice around a finger (or thumb), then using the hook to pull through a loop from the ball end of the yarn. Do not pull tight.

Hold the wrap flat between finger and thumb and work the starting chain(s), then work the required stitches into the wrap, working over the starting tail at the same time to enclose it. Then pull the starting tail gently to close the ring, and join with a slip stitch into the last of the starting chains.

## UNDERSTANDING ROUNDS

When working in rounds, the work is not turned, so the right side is always facing you. The stitches of the previous round face in the same direction as the stitches you are working, so the top of each stitch is always to the RIGHT of its stem.

## RING OF CHAINS

This method leaves a small hole at the center of the block, the size depending on the number of chains in the ring.

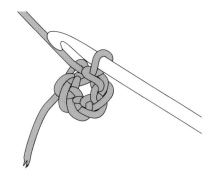

Work the required number of chains, then join into a circle with a slip stitch in the first chain made.

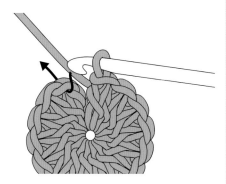

For each round, work the number of chains to stand for the first stitch, then work the required stitches into the center of the ring (not into the individual chains). You can work over the starting tail at the same time, to enclose it. Close the ring with a slip stitch in the top of the starting chains. Pull gently on the starting tail to neaten the center, and trim off the excess.

## FINISHING NEATLY

Always finish off each block securely; think ahead, and leave a long tail where it will be useful for sewing a seam. Where the edges of blocks will be hidden in a seam, simply work 1 chain, cut the yarn, and pull the tail through the last stitch. Where the edge will be visible in use, try this technique for a perfect finish:

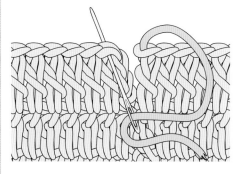

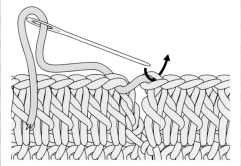

Do not work the final slip stitch of the last round. Cut the yarn leaving a 4 in (10 cm) tail and thread this into a yarn needle. Pass the needle under the top of the first stitch of the round as shown, and back through the last stitch. Darn in the tail on the wrong side.

## DARNING IN TAILS

Tails not enclosed during working a block may be darned in on the wrong side after completion. Use a yarn needle, and always darn in for at least 2 in (5 cm) to prevent the tail from slipping out again. For smooth, slippery yarns, reverse the direction and darn back again for a few stitches. Trim off the excess.

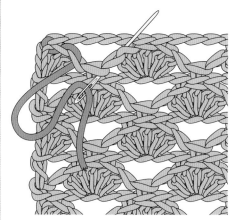

On lacy blocks, darn in the tails along the back of the stitches for about 2 in (5 cm), changing direction to suit the pattern, so that the tail will not show on the right side.

# BLOCK ARRANGEMENTS

Squares, diamonds, triangles, hexagons, and circles can be joined together in several different arrangements.

### SQUARES

Join squares into strips, then join the strips.

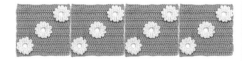

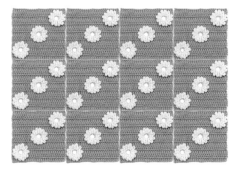

### HEXAGONS

Join hexagons into strips, then join the strips.

### DIAMONDS

Join diamonds into diagonally slanting strips, then join the strips.

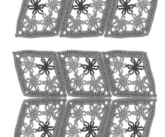

Alternatively, arrange blocks into sloping strips, then join the strips.

### TRIANGLES

Strips of triangles can be joined in two ways, as shown.

Six triangles can be joined to make a hexagon.

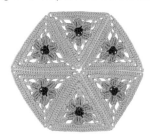

# CIRCLES

Circles may be fitted quite closely together, by joining just a few stitches at six points around each circle; join each circle in place in turn. The resulting gaps between the circles will be quite small.

Circles may also be joined into strips, and the strips joined together. The resulting gaps may be filled with small connector pieces, such as squares or circles formed by working the first one or two rounds of suitable blocks.

These Dahlia circles (block 70, page 123) are joined using the joining with picots method (page 21), with a connector piece made by working rounds 1 and 2 of the Butterfly circle (block 73, page 126).

Other suitable connectors may be contrived by working the first one or two rounds of many of the blocks in this book, including round 1 of the Coral trellis square (gray sample, block 16, page 69) and rounds 1 and 2 of the Blossom square (jade sample, block 17, page 70).

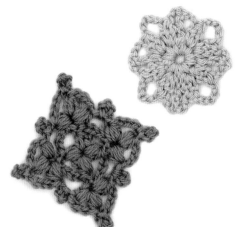

# JOINING BLOCKS

Blocks can be joined with sewn seams or crochet seams. Blocks made with picots on the last round are usually joined together as they are worked. All the blocks of the same shape in this book are of similar size, so that all the squares may be fitted together, or all the triangles, or all the diamonds, and so on.

## BLOCKING

Blocking your crochet pieces before joining them together will improve the neatness of the stitches and help the blocks to retain their shape. To retain the texture of crochet blocks, cold water blocking is recommended. Blocks made with picots on the last round can be blocked after joining together.

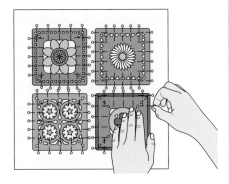

A blocking board is a small board (plywood or fiberboard) covered with a layer of batting and a layer of cotton fabric, which is pulled tight, folded over the edges, and stapled at the back. Checkered or gingham fabric provides a useful guide for square blocks.
1 Lay the blocks flat with right sides facing up.
2 To block, check the measurements with a ruler as you insert pins, gently easing the blocks into shape. Pin with large-headed pins at right angles to the edges, all around the edge of each block. Use as many pins as you need to hold the edges straight.
3 Use a spray bottle to mist the blocks thoroughly with cold water. Pat them gently to dampen all the stitches.
4 Allow to dry completely before removing the pins.

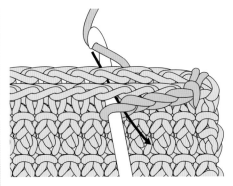

## SLIP STITCH SEAM

This firm seam is suitable for joining blocks worked in any direction. Working on the wrong side in matching yarn gives a neat appearance on the right side.
1 Place the two blocks right sides together.
2 Use a hook one size smaller than used for the blocks and (if possible) matching yarn. Insert the hook through both layers. On top/bottom edges, insert through matching stitches; on side edges, insert either one whole stitch in from each edge, or through the center of the first stitch of each layer. Pull through a loop of yarn.
3 Continue in slip stitch through both layers together.
When joining side edges of blocks worked in rows, try out a short length of seam to find a suitable spacing for the stitches. For example, when joining rows of double crochet, 2 slip stitches per row usually gives a neat result.
When working a zigzag seam (such as when joining hexagons), work 1 or 2 chains at each corner, so that the seam is not too tight.

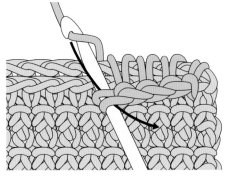

## SINGLE CROCHET SEAM

This seam is suitable for joining blocks worked in any direction. It may be worked on the wrong side, or on the right side as a decorative feature. When joining blocks of different colors, the seams may be worked all in one contrasting color for a unifying effect (see Busy Lizzie throw, pages 134–135).
1 Place the blocks right (or wrong) sides together.
2 Use a hook one size smaller than used for the blocks, and matching or contrasting yarn. Insert the hook through both layers—either through matching stitches, or through matching row ends—and pull through a loop.
3 Continue in single crochet through both layers together, joining each pair of stitches with 1 single crochet.
On side edges, try out a short length to find a suitable spacing, as for slip stitch seam.
At the corners of a zigzag seam, work 1 or 2 extra single crochet into the chain spaces of the intersection.
Neaten your yarn tails of any color by enclosing them as you work this seam.

## JOINING WITH PICOTS

Some blocks are worked with picots on the outer edges, which are designed to be joined together as work progresses. The blocks are only joined where corresponding picots meet, giving an open, lacy effect.

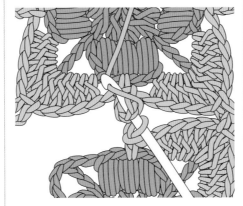

1 Work the first block as given in the instructions.
2 Then work the second block as far as the first picot to be joined, and work to the central chain of the picot—for example, on a 5-ch picot, work 2 ch.
3 With right side of first block facing up, insert the hook from below, through the center of the corresponding picot, and work a slip stitch, which counts as 1 chain (see diagram, left).
4 Complete the picot, then continue the final round of the second block to the next picot to be joined.
5 Repeat steps 3 and 4 as required, then complete the final round of the second block, and fasten off.

**Where several blocks meet together,** insert the hook into the picot diagonally opposite (see photo, below).

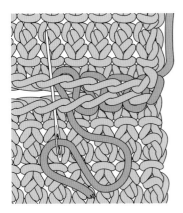

## FLAT SEWN SEAM

This seam is particularly suitable for blocks worked in the round, where the outer edges consist entirely of the tops of stitches. As you finish each block, you can leave a long yarn tail to use for seaming, thereby avoiding extra yarn tails to darn in.

1 Place the blocks on a flat surface with wrong sides (or right sides, if preferred) facing up.
2 Using a yarn needle, secure the yarn at the right (or use the tail from the block).
3 Link the two edges together as shown by passing the needle away from you, under one thread from each edge, then toward you, again under one thread from each edge. Do not pull too tightly.
4 At the end of the seam, secure with a small backstitch, and darn in the tail.

A similar seam may be worked to join the side edges of blocks worked in rows. Pass the needle under just one thread of the outermost stitch of each layer.

# EDGINGS

There are two methods of adding an edging to your work:
grown-on edgings and sewn-on borders.

## GROWN-ON EDGINGS

Grown-on edgings are worked directly on the edge of the crochet, and almost always begin with a row or round of single crochet, as below. For a neat, firm result, use a hook one size smaller than used for the blocks.

When working on a large project, it is advisable to try out a short length of edging, including a corner or two, to make sure the edging lies flat. If the edging is wavy, there are too many stitches, but if it curls inward, there are too few.

See page 24 for three grown-on edging samples.

## GROWN-ON SINGLE CROCHET BORDER

See the border used for the Busy Lizzie throw (pages 134—135), which is worked in rounds of single crochet, increasing at outer corners and decreasing at inward corners, with the final round in reverse rope stitch edging.

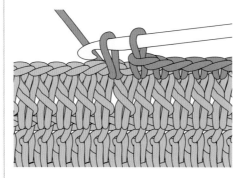

### SINGLE CROCHET ON AN OUTER, TOP, OR BOTTOM EDGE

On the outer edge of a block worked in the round, or on the top edge of a block worked in rows, work 1 sc into each stitch as shown. On the lower edge of a block worked in rows, work 1 sc in the base of each stitch.

On the outer edge of a circle, you may need to increase a few stitches to keep the edge flat—about 8 sts for a full circle.

Where an edge includes chain spaces, try working 1 sc into the space for each chain; you may need to adjust the number slightly.

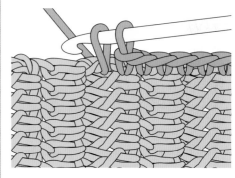

### SINGLE CROCHET ON A SIDE EDGE

On a side edge of a block worked in rows, insert the hook under two threads of the first (or last) stitch of each row, and try out a short length to test the number of stitches required for a flat result, according to these guidelines:

**Rows of sc:** 1 sc in side edge of each row.
**Rows of hdc:** 3 sc in side edge of every 2 rows.
**Rows of dc:** 2 sc in side edge of every row.
**Rows of tr:** 3 sc in side edge of each row.

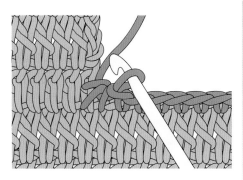

## SINGLE CROCHET AT INWARD CORNERS

At inward corners, it is necessary to decrease on every round to keep the edge flat.

**At a right angle:** Decrease by 2 sc on every round, by working 3 sc tog, with the central insertion exactly in the corner. On subsequent rounds, work 3 sc tog, with the central insertion in the previous 3 sc tog, or work 2 sc tog, inserting the hook in the sc before and after the previous decrease.

**At a wide angle:** Decrease by 2 sc as for a right angle, but not on every round.

**At a sharp angle:** Decrease by 4 sc, working 3 sc tog at either side of the corner, on every round or every second or third round, as required.

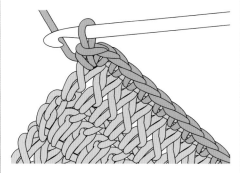

## SINGLE CROCHET AT OUTER CORNERS

At outer corners of a square, increase by working 3 sc, or [1 sc, 1 ch, 1 sc], in the same place on every round.

The outer corners of other shapes are not right angles, so if you want a wide border all in single crochet, you may need to experiment:

**At the corners of a triangle:** 5 sc, or [1 sc, 3 ch, 1 sc], or [2 sc, 1 ch, 2 sc].

**At the corners of a hexagon:** 3 sc on the first round. If worked on every round, this will make a slightly wavy edge, so for a wide border work every second or third round with no increasing.

**At the corners of a diamond:** Work the sharp top and bottom corners as for a triangle, and the other corners as for a square.

## SEWN-ON BORDERS

These are normally worked sideways—that is, beginning with a short side—and to the length required. The length can then be adjusted to fit exactly when the border is sewn in place. See page 25 for three sewn-on border samples.

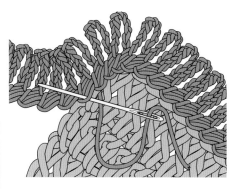

## FITTING A SEWN-ON BORDER

Work the border to the length you think you need, and slip the working loop onto a split marker to prevent unraveling. Pin the border in place with safety pins. Butt the two edges together and join with a flat sewn seam (or a crochet seam if you prefer). This knotted loop edging (page 25) fits easily around corners, but if necessary, gather the border slightly at outer corners, so it is not stretched. Before you seam the last few inches, adjust the length to fit exactly. Join the two ends of the border with a flat sewn seam.

## SMALL PICOT EDGING

This edging is worked lengthwise, usually as the final row of a single crochet border.

With right side of work facing, work a few rows or rounds of single crochet (2 rows shown on chart).
**Small picot row (chart row 3):** 1 ch, skip first sc, * 3 ch, ss in first of these 3 ch, skip 1 sc, 1 sc in next sc, * repeat from * to * to end, working last sc in 1 ch. Fasten off. To complete a round, ss in first ch.
**Notes:**
• At outer corners, try working [3 ch, ss in first of these 3 ch, 1 sc in next sc] twice, exactly at the corner, to enable the edging to lie flat.
• At inward corners, work 2 (or 3) sc tog exactly at the corner.
• If working in rounds, any number of rounds of sc may precede the Small picot row.

## PLAIN RUFFLE

This edging is worked lengthwise, and may begin with any number of stitches.

With right side of work facing, work 1 row or round of single crochet (1 row shown on chart).
**Row 2:** 1 ch, 1 sc in first sc, 2 sc in each sc, ending 2 sc in 1 ch.
**Row 3:** As row 2. Fasten off.
**Notes:**
• This edging may also be worked in rounds, increasing on each round in the same way.
• For a wider, looser ruffle work rows 2 and 3 in dc or tr. For a tighter ruffle, repeat row 3 once more.
• At outer corners, work 3 sc in the same place on the first 2 rows of sc. At inward corners, work 3 sc tog on the first 2 rows of sc (see page 23).

## BLOCK EDGING

Worked lengthwise, this bold edging is quick and simple to work.

With right side of work facing, begin at right and work a few rows or rounds of single crochet (2 rows shown on chart).
**Block row (chart row 3):** 3 ch, skip 3 sc, * 1 dc in next sc, 3 ch, 4 dc in sp behind dc just made, skip 3 sc, * repeat from * to * to last sc, 3 ch, ss in last st. Fasten off. If working in rounds, end with 1 block of 3 dc, ss in first dc of round.
**Notes:**
• At outer corners, adjust the number of sc so that each edge has a multiple of 4 sts, plus 1—the extra st should be the center st of 3 at each corner (see page 23). On Block row, work 1 dc (carrying a block) into the center sc of 3 at each corner.
• To work in rounds, work 2 or more rounds of sc, ending with a multiple of 4 sts. Work 3rd round as Block row, ending 1 dc in base of 3 ch at beg of round, 4 dc in sp behind dc just made. Fasten off.

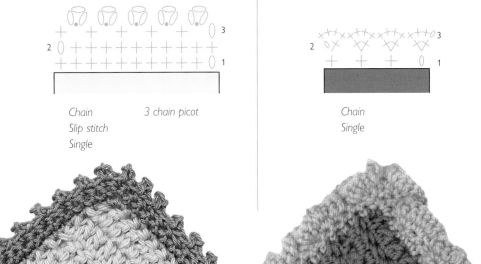

*Chain*       *3 chain picot*
*Slip stitch*
*Single*

*Chain*
*Single*

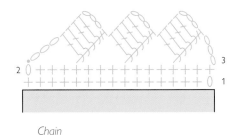

*Chain*
*Slip stitch*       *Double*       *Double around stem*
*Single*

# FRILLED FLOWERS

This edging is worked sideways and sewn in place.

Make 5 ch, join into a ring with ss in first ch.
**Row 1:** 3 ch, 7 dc into ring, turn.
**Row 2:** 3 ch, skip first dc, * [1 sc in next dc, 3 ch] 6 times, 1 sc in 3rd of 3 ch, 9 ch, ss in 5th ch from hook (making another ring), turn.
**Row 3:** 3 ch, 7 dc into ring, 1 ch, ss in last 3-ch loop of previous repeat, turn.
**Row 4:** 1 ch, work as row 2 from * to end.
Repeat rows 3 and 4 to required length, ending row 4 by omitting the final 9 ch and ss.
Notes:
• At outer corners, arrange the edging so that a join between 2 repeats falls exactly at the corner.
• At inward corners, work 14 ch instead of 9 ch on row 4, so that one repeat can be placed on either side of the corner.

# DOUBLE SHELLS

Worked sideways, this edging is worked separately and sewn in place.

**Row 1:** 4 ch, 1 dc in first ch made. (1 ring made)
**Row 2:** 3 ch, [2 dc, 2 ch, 3 dc] into ring (1 double shell made), turn.
**Row 3:** 5 ch, * [ss, 3 ch, 1 dc] into 2-ch sp at top of double shell (1 ring made), turn.
**Row 4:** 3 ch, [2 dc, 2 ch, 3 dc] into ring, 1 dc in 3rd of 5 ch at beg of previous row, turn.
Repeat rows 3 and 4 to length required.
Fasten off.
Notes:
• At outer corners, work to length required, ending with row 4.
**Next row:** 3 ch, work as row 3 from * to end.
**Foll row:** As row 4, ending ss in dc at base of 3 ch, turn. Continue in pattern, beginning with row 3.

# KNOTTED LOOPS

Worked sideways, this edging is worked separately and sewn in place. It fits easily around corners.

**Special abbreviation**
**PS (puff stitch):** [Yrh, insert as given, pull through a loop] 3 times in same place, yrh, pull through first 6 loops on hook, yrh, pull through remaining 2 loops on hook.

**Row 1:** 13 ch, PS in first ch made. Do not turn the work.
**Row 2:** 12 ch, PS in top of previous PS (inserting the hook under two threads), do not turn.
Repeat row 2 to length required. Fasten off.
Note:
The length of the fringe may be adjusted by working more or fewer chains.

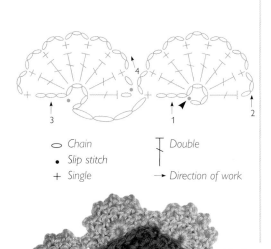

- ⬭ Chain
- • Slip stitch
- + Single

- ⊤ Double
- → Direction of work

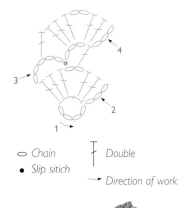
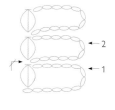

- ⬭ Chain
- • Slip sititch

- ⊤ Double
- → Direction of work

- ⬭ Chain
- ⬗ Puff stitch

- ↗ Do not turn
- → Direction of work

# PLANNING A PROJECT

Your starting point for a project may be a favorite block, an exciting color combination, a new yarn you want to try out, or a gift needed for a special occasion. Whatever your inspiration, there are several factors to take into account when planning a project: the block(s), the yarn, the colors, the arrangement, and the method of construction. Follow these guidelines for a successful result.

## CHOOSE THE BLOCK(S)

Crochet fabric can be smooth, lacy, or textured, depending on which technique you are using.

Consider the use of the finished item to help you choose a suitable block, for example:

**A winter scarf** may be lacy or quite solid, but the wrong side of the blocks will be visible in wear. The wrong sides of some blocks are similar in appearance to the right sides, while others may differ considerably.

**A blanket** for a new baby should not be too lacy, as tiny fingers can become trapped in the holes.

**A shopping bag** requires sturdy blocks, without large holes (unless you choose to add a lining).

Smooth blocks are solid and have greater strength than lacy or textured blocks. Interest can be added by using different colors and motifs.

Lacy blocks work well when they are combined with each other, but they can also be used to add a touch of lightness to other block combinations.

Textured blocks add surface interest and three-dimensionality to designs.

## CHOOSE THE YARN

Consider the properties you need for the project you are planning in order to choose your yarn, for example:

**For a winter scarf,** a warm, light, soft yarn might be your choice, such as merino wool or angora blends.

**For a lacy wrap,** a smooth, satiny yarn such as glazed cotton, viscose, or silk will drape well and show off the stitch textures.

**For a baby blanket,** a machine-washable yarn is a practical choice.

**For a shopping bag,** a strong, hard-wearing yarn is required, such as cotton or cotton/synthetic blends.

Also consider the weight of the yarn. This will affect the size of blocks you make (see pages 12–13), which in turn will affect the finished design: bold and chunky, or light and delicate.

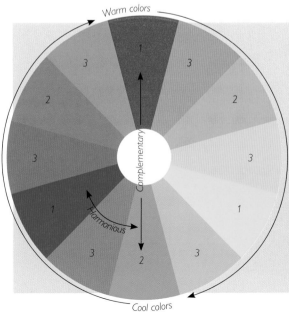

## COLOR WHEEL

You can use an artist's color wheel to help you choose colors that go together.

The color wheel is made of three primary colors (1): red, blue, and yellow. These are mixed in pairs to create the secondary colors: (2) purple, green, and orange. These in turn are mixed with their neighbors to create tertiary colors (3).

Opposite colors on the wheel (such as green and red) are "complementary" colors.

Adjacent colors on the wheel are harmonious—for example, blue, turquoise, and green.

# CHOOSE THE COLORS

Color choice is ultimately a matter of personal taste, but may also be influenced by the nature of the project:

**For accessories,** match or contrast colors for scarves, wraps, purses, or bags to coordinate with your wardrobe.

**For a pillow or throw,** choose colors to suit the color scheme of a room—either subtly blending with the scheme, or brightly contrasting, to provide an exciting focal point.

You may come across a color combination you really like, perhaps in a fabric print or a picture. You can take photographs, or keep a sketchbook or scrapbook, for future reference.

## WARM COLORS

Colors on the orange side of the color wheel, from yellow through red, are warm colors. Choose these for bright, cheerful impact.

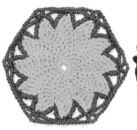

## COOL COLORS

Cool colors are those on the blue side of the color wheel, from lilac through green. These colors have a calming effect.

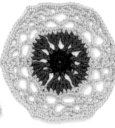

## COMPLEMENTARY COLORS

Used together, complementary colors create vibrant, contrasting combinations. Choose slightly softened shades for a rich, rather than clashing, result.

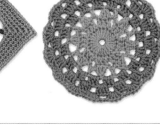

## HARMONIOUS COLORS

Harmonious colors can be used to enhance one another. Adding a neutral can bring out the subtle differences in hue.

## TEST STRIPS

Use yarn from your stash (or buy small skeins of tapestry wool) to try out color combinations. Wind yarns around a strip of cardboard and secure with adhesive tape. The proportions of the stripes can be varied, as well as the colors. Such a strip can then be used as a shopping guide when purchasing yarn.

## CHOOSE THE ARRANGEMENT

The blocks in this book can be combined in many different ways. Some of the basic arrangements are shown on pages 18–19.

All the blocks of the same shape in this book are of similar size—that is, all the squares may be fitted together, or all the triangles, or all the diamonds, and so on. The mix and matches dotted throughout the book are just some of the ways in which the blocks can be combined and are designed to inspire you to create your own arrangements.

Always make sample blocks to try out the yarns and colors you have chosen, to make sure you are happy with the result. Also note down the hook size used for each block. Block each sample as on page 20.

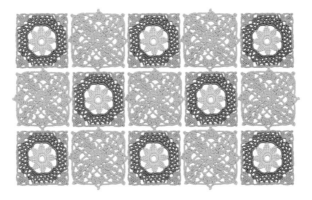

You can choose two or more block designs of the same shape and put them together in various arrangements.

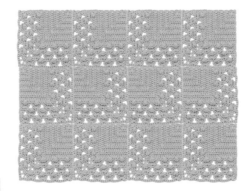

Some blocks feature directional rather than symmetrical designs. These blocks may be arranged in various ways to make larger patterns.

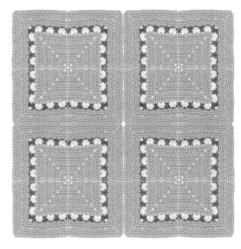

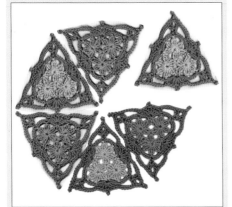

### DESIGN TIP

With the aid of a photocopier and a camera, you can quickly try out different arrangements by photocopying sample blocks and arranging the copies in different ways. You can then photograph the different arrangements and decide what works best.

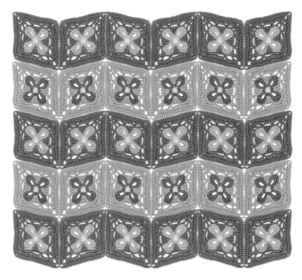

You can make the same block in more than one color combination, and arrange them to make larger patterns, such as these zigzag stripes formed with diamonds. See also the Busy Lizzie throw on pages 134–135.

# PLAN THE CONSTRUCTION

Measure your sample block(s) as page on 12.

1 Decide on the finished size of the project and the size of each section (such as front, back, and side/base panels of a bag).

2 Draw a plan of the arrangement—graph paper is useful for this.

3 Count how many blocks will you need for each section.

4 Decide on the order in which you will make the blocks, how you will join them (see pages 20–21) and any edging required (see pages 22–25).

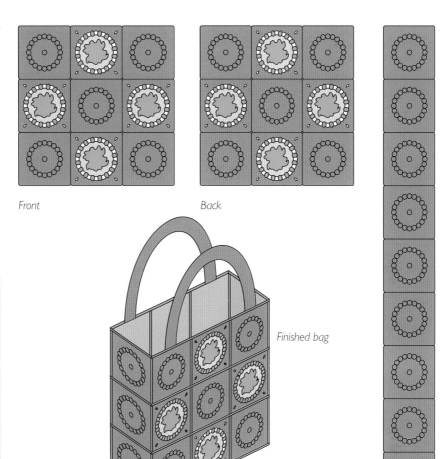

Front

Back

Finished bag

Sides and base

## LOOKING AFTER CROCHET

Always clean crochet regularly, according to the care instructions on the ball band of the yarns you have used. You may prefer to have large throws and afghans professionally dry-cleaned.

To store articles not in use, never enclose them in a plastic bag, as the fibers will not be able to breathe and the static cling created by polythene will attract dust and dirt. Instead, wrap in a clean cotton pillowcase or sheet, depending on size. Store in a dry, cool, dust-free place, adding a bag of dried lavender to keep the crochet smelling sweet and to deter moths.

## CALCULATE THE YARN REQUIRED

The most accurate way to calculate the yarn you will need for a large project is to make a block, unravel it, and measure the length of each color used. You can then use the yardage given on the yarn ball band to estimate how many balls of each color will be required for the number of blocks you want. Repeat for each design of block you intend to use.

To calculate the amount of yarn required for an edging (especially on a large article, such as a throw), work a short length of edging over, say, three or four blocks, unravel it, and measure the length of yarn used. You can then estimate how much will be required for the whole edging.

Be generous when estimating the total for each color—it's better to have yarn left over than to need another ball, and find you can't buy the matching dye lot.

# 2
# DIRECTORY OF BLOCKS

The Directory is a showcase of the over 75 beautiful designs that are featured in this book. Organized into four color themes—spring green, sky blue, summer pink, harvest gold—it contains a mix of shapes and skill levels. Flick through this colorful visual guide, select your design, and then turn to the relevant page of instructions to create your chosen piece.

# SPRING GREEN

A delightful collection of spring flower designs for you to pick from. With single blooms and intricate arrangements, the palette is created in pale greens, yellows, and blues, evoking the delicate blossoming of spring.

**28** DAISY CHAIN SQUARE

**8** JONQUIL TRIANGLE

**54** DAFFODIL HEXAGON

**64** SPRING MEADOW HEXAGON

**24** CROCUS SQUARE

**26** PRIMROSE SQUARE

**7** SHAMROCK
TRIANGLE

23 LACY DAISY SQUARE

41 KINGCUP DIAMOND

50 SNOWDROP HEXAGON

63 SWIRLING HEXAGON

**36** TULIP SQUARE

**10** VIOLET TRIANGLE

**75** BUTTERCUP CIRCLE

**39** FILET FLOWER SQUARE

**17** BLOSSOM SQUARE

**40** DANDELION DIAMOND

**67** ROSETTE CIRCLE

**9** LILY TRIANGLE

**2** INTARSIA PETAL TRIANGLE

**76** DANDELION CIRCLE

**35** BOBBLE SQUARE

**60** BOBBLE FLOWER HEXAGON

# SKY BLUE

As spring turns into summer, the days get longer and lighter and the sky gets bluer. Pick a subtle combination of different shades of blue or make the colors pop by adding oranges and pinks.

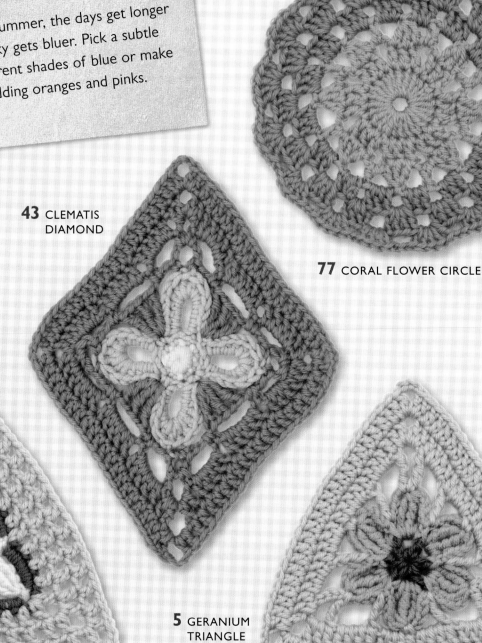

**43** CLEMATIS DIAMOND

**77** CORAL FLOWER CIRCLE

**6** WINDFLOWER TRIANGLE

**5** GERANIUM TRIANGLE

**48** CORNFLOWER HEXAGON

**15** STAR FLOWER SQUARE

**19** THREE DAISY SQUARE

**47** LARGE FLOWER HEXAGON

**18** BUTTERFLY SQUARE

**44** FOUR DAISY DIAMOND

**74** POPCORN FLOWER CIRCLE

**27** IRISH ROSE SQUARE

**12** MICHAELMAS DAISY TRIANGLE

**53** SPIRAL WINDFLOWER HEXAGON

**20** EMBOSSED FLOWER SQUARE

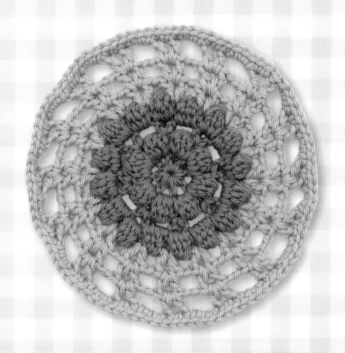

**78** BOBBLE FLOWER CIRCLE

# SUMMER PINK

The fun and heat of summer is evoked by these vibrant pinks, set off by leafy greens and cool neutrals. The abundance of summer flowers is reflected by the number of representational blocks.

**31** SPANISH POPPY SQUARE

**49** FRILLED FLOWER HEXAGON

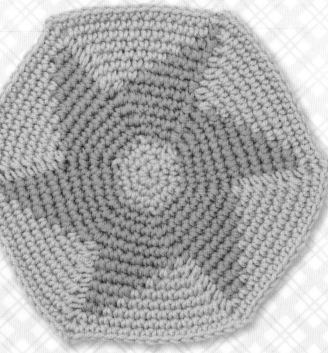

**46** COLORWORK HEXAGON

**13** FLORETTE TRIANGLE

**14** GRANNY ROSE SQUARE

**45** ASTER DIAMOND

**51** OLD FRENCH
ROSE HEXAGON

**38** ROSEBUD SQUARE

**55** BUSY LIZZIE HEXAGON

**72** PENNY FLOWER CIRCLE

**4** GRANNY ROSE TRIANGLE

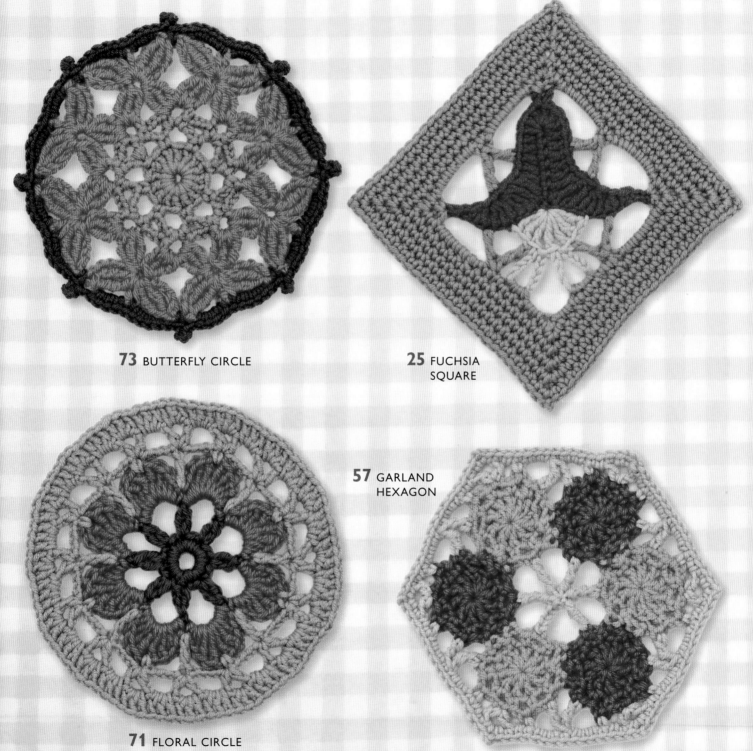

**73** BUTTERFLY CIRCLE

**25** FUCHSIA SQUARE

**57** GARLAND HEXAGON

**71** FLORAL CIRCLE

**56** WILD ROSE HEXAGON

**58** LOOPY FLOWER HEXAGON

**16** CORAL TRELLIS SQUARE

**3** CENTAURY TRIANGLE

**32** RUFFLED FLOWER SQUARE

**69** THISTLE CIRCLE

**52** DIANTHUS HEXAGON

**37** OFF-CENTER SQUARE

# HARVEST GOLD

Fall is one of the most colorful seasons of all, with leaves turning red, orange, yellow, and gold. Embrace these warm tones to make cozy blankets in preparation for winter.

**42** IRISH DIAMOND

**66** HELENIUM CIRCLE

**1** CELTIC FLOWER TRIANGLE

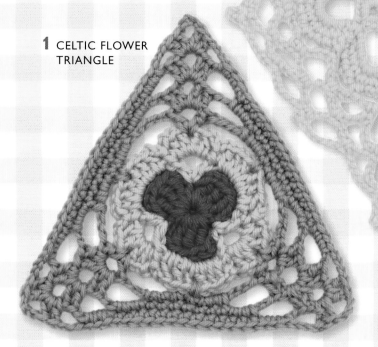

**61** OPEN FLOWER HEXAGON

**62** SPINNING DAHLIA HEXAGON

**33** STONECROP SQUARE

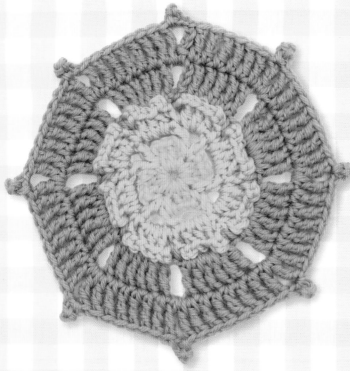

**68** CELTIC FLOWER CIRCLE

**21** CELTIC FLOWER SQUARE

**59** STAR FLOWER HEXAGON

**30** SNEEZEWORT SQUARE

**29** POPPY SQUARE

**70** DAHLIA CIRCLE

**11** STONECROP TRIANGLE

**34** SUNFLOWER SQUARE

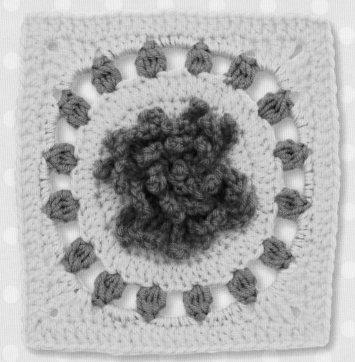

**22** CHRYSANTHEMUM SQUARE

**65** OPEN DAHLIA HEXAGON

# 3
# INSTRUCTIONS

In this chapter you'll find a written pattern and a chart for every design. The blocks are organized by shape to enable easy mixing and matching, as all the blocks of the same shape are the same size.

# CELTIC FLOWER TRIANGLE
*directory view page 48*

A B C

**Skill level:** intermediate
**Method of working:** in the round

**Key:**
◯ Chain
• Slip stitch
+ Single
╥ Double
╤ Treble

▷ Start/join in new color
◀ Fasten off

## METHOD

Using A, make 4 ch, join into a ring with ss in first ch.

**Round 1:** 4 ch, [3 tr into ring, 3 ch, 1 sc into ring, 3 ch] twice, 3 tr into ring, 3 ch, ss in first of 4 ch. 3 petals. Fasten off A. Join B to any sc between petals.

**Round 2:** 6 ch, 1 dc in same place, [5 ch, sk 1 petal, [1 dc, 3 ch, 1 dc] in next sc] twice, 5 ch, sk 1 petal, ss in 3rd of 6 ch.

**Round 3:** 3 ch, * [2 dc, 1 ch, 2 dc] in next 3-ch sp, 2 ch, 1 sc in next dc, 2 ch, [3 dc, 1 ch, 3 dc] in 5-ch sp, 2 ch, # 1 sc in next dc, 2 ch, * rep from * to * once more, then once again from * to #, ss in first of 3 ch. 6 petals: 3 small, 3 large. Fasten off B. Join C to 1-ch sp at center of any small petal.

**Round 4:** 6 ch, 1 dc in same place, * 7 ch, 1 sc in 1-ch sp at center of next (large) petal, 7 ch, # [1 dc, 3 ch, 1 dc] in 1-ch sp at center of next (small) petal, * rep from * to * once more, then once again from * to #, ss in 3rd of 6 ch.

**Round 5:** Ss into 3-ch sp, 6 ch, 2 dc in same place, * 5 ch, 3 sc in next 5-ch sp, 1 sc in next sc, 3 sc in next 5-ch sp, 5 ch, # [2 dc, 3 ch, 2 dc] in next 3-ch sp, * rep from * to * once more, then once again from * to #, 1 dc in first ch sp, ss in 3rd of 6 ch.

**Round 6:** Ss into 3-ch sp, 6 ch, 2 dc in same place, * 5 ch, 3 sc in next 5-ch sp, 1 sc in each of 7 sc, 3 sc in next 5-ch sp, 5 ch, # [2 dc, 3 ch, 2 dc] in next 3-ch sp, * rep from * to * once more, then once again from * to #, 1 dc in first ch sp, ss in 3rd of 6 ch.

**Round 7:** Ss into 3-ch sp, 6 ch, 2 dc in same place, * 3 ch, 3 sc in 5-ch sp, 1 sc in each of 13 sc, 3 sc in 5-ch sp, 3 ch, # [2 dc, 3 ch, 2 dc] in next 3-ch sp, * rep from * to * once more, then once again from * to #, 1 dc in first ch sp, ss in 3rd of 6 ch. Fasten off C.

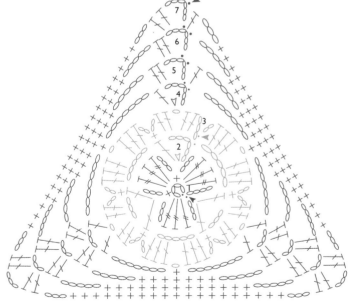

# 2 INTARSIA PETAL TRIANGLE
*directory view page 37*

A B C

**Skill level:** easy
**Method of working:**
in rows

**Key:**
⟋ *Chain*
T *Double*

▷ *Start/join in new color*
◀ *Fasten off*

## METHOD

**Special abbreviation**

**chg to B (or C):** changing to B (or C) for the final "yrh, pull through" of the last st worked.

Using A, make 4 ch.
**Row 1:** 2 dc in 4th ch from hook. 3 sts.
**Row 2:** 3 ch, 1 dc in first dc, 1 dc in next dc, 2 dc in 3rd of 3 ch. 5 sts. Fasten off A. Join B to same place.
**Row 3:** 3 ch, 1 dc in first dc, 1 dc in each dc, 2 dc in 3rd of 3 ch. 7 sts.
**Rows 4–5:** As row 3. 11 sts.
Join C to top of last dc of row 5. Do not fasten off B.
On rows 6–10, work in 2 colors, enclosing the color not in use until it is required.
**Row 6:** In C, 3 ch, 1 dc in first dc chg to B; in B, 1 dc in each of next 9 dc chg to C; in C, 2 dc in 3rd of 3 ch. 13 sts.
**Row 7:** In C, 3 ch, 1 dc in first dc, 1 dc in each of next 2 dc chg to B; in B, 1 dc in each of next 7 dc chg to C; in C, 1 dc in each of 2 dc, 2 dc in 3rd of 3 ch. 15 sts.

**Row 8:** In C, 3 ch, 1 dc in first dc, 1 dc in each of next 4 dc chg to B; in B, 1 dc in each of next 5 dc chg to C; in C, 1 dc in each of 4 dc, 2 dc in 3rd of 3 ch. 17 sts.
**Row 9:** In C, 3 ch, 1 dc in first dc, 1 dc in each of next 6 dc chg to B; in B, 1 dc in each of next 3 dc chg to C; in C, 1 dc in each of 6 dc, 2 dc in 3rd of 3 ch. 19 sts.
**Row 10:** In C, 3 ch, 1 dc in first dc, 1 dc in each of next 8 dc chg to B; in B, 1 dc in next dc chg to C; in C, 1 dc in each of 8 dc, 2 dc in 3rd of 3 ch. 21 sts.
Fasten off B. Continue in C.
**Rows 11–13:** As row 3. 25 sts.
Fasten off C.

Six of these blocks can be joined to form a hexagon, making a six-petalled flower.

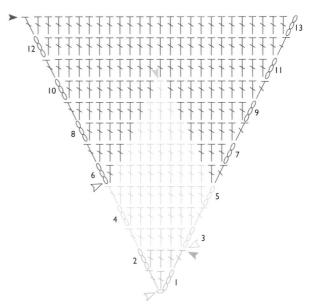

# 3 CENTAURY TRIANGLE
*directory view page 46*

A B

**Skill level:** advanced
**Method of working:** in the round

**Key:**

| | | | |
|---|---|---|---|
| ⬯ | Fingerwrap | ⑂ | 2 trebles together |
| ⌒ | Chain | | |
| • | Slip stitch | | 3 trebles together |
| + | Single | | |
| ⊤ | Double | ▷ | Start/join in new color |
| ⟂ | Treble | ◀ | Fasten off |

## METHOD

Using A, make a fingerwrap.

**Round 1:** 3 ch, 2 tr tog into wrap, [10 ch, 3 tr tog into wrap] twice, 10 ch, ss in ch closing 2 tr tog. 3 petals.

**Round 2:** 3 ch, [2 tr tog, 4 ch, 3 tr tog, 4 ch, 3 tr tog, 4 ch, 2 tr tog] in same place as base of first 3 ch, * ss in 10-ch sp (first flower made), [2 tr tog, 4 ch, 3 tr tog, 4 ch, 3 tr tog, 4 ch, 3 tr tog, 4 ch, 2 tr tog] in ch closing next petal, * rep from * to * once more, ss in 10-ch sp, 2 tr tog in center of first flower, 4 ch, ss in ch closing first 2 tr tog of round. Fasten off A. Join B to 4-ch sp before any corner petal.

**Round 3:** 6 ch, ss in 5th ch from hook, * sk 1 petal, 4 sc in next 4-ch sp, 1 ch, sk 1 petal, 4 sc in next 4-ch sp, sk 1 petal, 1 sc in ss between petals, sk 1 petal, 4 sc in next ch sp, 1 ch, sk 1 petal, 4 sc in 4-ch sp, # 5 ch, ss in 5th ch from hook, * rep from * to * once more, then once again from * to #, ss in first of 6 ch.

**Round 4:** Ss in 5-ch picot, 6 ch, 2 dc in same picot, * 6 ch, sk 4 sc, 1 sc in 1-ch sp, 1 ch, sk 4 sc, [2 dc, 1 ch, 2 dc] in next sc, 1 ch, sk 4 sc, 1 sc in 1-ch sp, 6 ch, sk 4 sc, # [2 dc, 3 ch, 2 dc] in 5-ch picot, * rep from * to * once more, then once again from * to #, 1 dc in first ch sp, ss in 3rd of 6 ch.

**Round 5:** Ss into 3-ch sp, 7 ch, ss in 5th ch from hook, 1 ch, 1 sc in same place, * 1 sc in each of 2 dc, 6 sc in 6-ch sp, sk 1 sc, 1 sc in 1-ch sp, 1 sc in each of 2 dc, 1 sc in 1-ch sp, 3 ch, ss in last sc made, 1 sc in each of 2 dc, 1 sc in 1-ch sp, sk 1 sc, 6 sc in 6-ch sp, 1 sc in each of 2 dc, # [1 sc, 6 ch, ss in 5th ch from hook, 1 ch, 1 sc] in 3-ch sp, * rep from * to * once more, then once again from * to #, ss in first of 7 ch. Fasten off B.

# GRANNY ROSE TRIANGLE
*directory view page 44*

A  B

**Skill level:** easy
**Method of working:**
in the round

**Key:**

⌒  *Chain*

·  *Slip stitch*

+  *Single*

T  *Half double*

Ŧ  *Double*

Ŧ  *Double in stitch below*

▷  *Start/join in new color*

◄  *Fasten off*

## METHOD

Using A, make 8 ch, join into a ring with ss in first ch.

**Round 1:** 5 ch, [3 dc into ring, 2 ch] 5 times, 2 dc into ring, ss in 3rd of 5 ch. 6 petals made.

**Round 2:** Ss into 2-ch sp, 5 ch, [1 sc in next 2-ch sp, 4 ch] 5 times, ss in first of 5 ch.

**Round 3:** Ss into 4-ch sp, 3 ch, [2 dc, 2 ch, 3 dc] in same ch sp, * [3 dc, 2 ch, 3 dc] in next 2-ch sp, * rep from * to * 4 more times, ss in 3rd of 3 ch.
Fasten off A. Join B to any 2-ch sp.

**Round 4:** 6 ch, 4 dc in same ch sp, * 1 dc between next 2 groups of 3 dc, 1 dc in sc of round 2 below this space, 1 hdc between same 2 groups, 2 ch, 1 sc in next 2-ch sp, 2 ch, 1 hdc between next 2 groups, 1 dc in sc below, 1 dc between same 2 groups, # [4 dc, 3 ch, 4 dc] in next 2-ch sp, * rep from * to * once more, then once again from * to #, 3 dc in same sp as beg of round, ss in 3rd of 6 ch.

**Round 5:** Ss into 3-ch sp, 4 ch, 1 sc in same ch sp, * 4 ch, 1 sc in space between next 2 groups, 5 ch, 2 sc tog over [next and foll 2-ch sps], 5 ch, 1 sc between next 2 groups, 4 ch, # [1 sc, 3 ch, 1 sc] in 2-ch sp at corner, * rep from * to * once more, then once again from * to #, ss in first of 4 ch.

**Round 6:** Ss into 3-ch sp, 4 ch, 1 sc in same ch sp, * 4 ch, 1 sc in 4-ch sp, [5 ch, 1 sc in 5-ch sp] twice, 5 ch, 1 sc in 4-ch sp, 4 ch, # [1 sc, 3 ch, 1 sc] in 3-ch sp at corner, * rep from * to * once more, then once again from * to #, ss in first of 4 ch.

**Round 7:** Ss into 3-ch sp, 4 ch, 1 sc in same ch sp, * 4 sc in 4-ch sp, [5 sc in 5-ch sp] 3 times, 4 sc in 4-ch sp, # [1 sc, 2 ch, 1 sc] in 3-ch sp at corner, * rep from * to * once more, then once again from * to #, ss in first of 3 ch. 25 sc on each side.
Fasten off B.

## 5 GERANIUM TRIANGLE
*directory view page 38*

A B C

**Skill level:** easy
**Method of working:** in the round

**Key:**
- ⬭ Chain
- • Slip stitch
- Front-raised single
- Double
- Treble
- Double treble
- 3 double trebles together
- ▷ Start/join in new color
- ◀ Fasten off

## METHOD

**Special abbreviation**
**frsc (front raised sc):** inserting hook from front, work 1 sc around post of given stitch.

Using A, make 4 ch, join into a ring with ss in first ch.
**Round 1:** 5 ch, [1 dc into ring, 2 ch] 5 times, ss in 3rd of 5 ch. Fasten off A. Join B to any dc.
**Round 2:** 1 ch, * 5 ch, 3 dtr tog in next 2-ch sp, 5 ch, 1 frsc in next dc, * rep from * to * 5 more times, working last frsc in same place as beg of round. Fasten off B. Join C to any 3 dtr tog.
**Round 3:** 8 ch, 1 dtr in same st, * 3 ch, 1 tr in next frsc, 3 ch, 1 sc in next 3 dtr tog, 3 ch, 1 tr in next

frsc, 3 ch, # [1 dtr, 3 ch, 1 dtr] in next 3 dtr tog, * rep from * to * once more, then once again from * to #, ss in 5th of 8 ch.
**Round 4:** Ss into 3-ch sp, 6 ch, 2 dc in same sp, * [1 dc in next st, 3 dc in 3-ch sp] 4 times, 1 dc in next st, # [2 dc, 3 ch, 2 dc] in 3-ch sp at corner, * rep from * to * once more, then once again from * to #, ss in 3rd of 6 ch. 21 dc on each side.
**Round 5:** Ss into 3-ch sp, 6 ch, 2 dc in same sp, * 1 dc in each of 21 dc, [2 dc, 3 ch, 2 dc] in 3-ch sp, * rep from * to * once more, 1 dc in each of 21 dc, ss in 3rd of 6 ch. 25 dc on each side. Fasten off C.

### MIX AND MATCH: 5 + 6

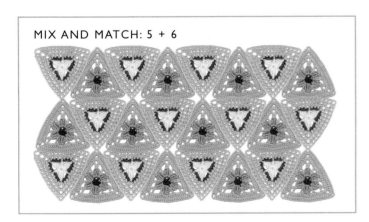

**6**

# WINDFLOWER TRIANGLE
*directory view page 38*

A  B  C

**Skill level:** easy
**Method of working:** in the round

**Key:**

| | | | |
|---|---|---|---|
| ⌒ | Chain | | |
| · | Slip stitch | | 3 trebles together |
| + | Single | ▷ | Start/join in new color |
| ⊤ | Double | ◀ | Fasten off |
| | 2 doubles together | | |

## METHOD

Using A, make 9 ch, join into a ring with ss in first ch.

**Round 1:** 3 ch, 2 tr tog into ring, [5 ch, 2 dc tog into ring, 5 ch, 3 tr tog into ring] twice, 5 ch, 2 dc tog into ring, 5 ch, ss in 2 tr tog at beg of round.
Fasten off A. Join B to 5-ch sp before any 3 tr tog.

**Round 2:** 4 ch, * sk 3 tr tog, 6 sc in next 5-ch sp, 1 ch, sk 2 dc tog, 6 sc in next 5-ch sp, # 3 ch, * rep from * to * once more, then once again from * to #, ss in first ch of round. 12 sc on each side.
Fasten off B. Join C to any 3-ch sp.

**Round 3:** 6 ch, 1 dc in same ch sp, 1 ch, * [1 dc in next sc, 1 ch, sk 1 sc] 3 times, 1 dc in 1-ch sp, [1 ch, sk 1 sc, 1 dc in next sc] 3 times, # [1 ch, 1 dc, 3 ch, 1 dc, 1 ch] in 3-ch sp, * rep from * to * once more, then once again from * to #, 1 ch, ss in 3rd of 6 ch.

**Round 4:** Ss into 3-ch sp, 6 ch, 1 dc in same ch sp, 1 ch, * [1 dc in next dc, 1 ch, sk 1 ch] 9 times, # [1 dc, 3 ch, 1 dc] in 3-ch sp, 1 ch, * rep from * to * once more, then once again from * to #, ss in 3rd of 6 ch.

**Round 5:** Ss into 3-ch sp, 6 ch, 1 dc in same ch sp, 1 ch, * [1 dc in next dc, 1 ch, sk 1 ch] 11 times, # [1 dc, 3 ch, 1 dc] in 3-ch sp, 1 ch, * rep from * to * once more, then once again from * to #, ss in 3rd of 6 ch. 12 ch sps on each side, plus corner sps.
Fasten off C.

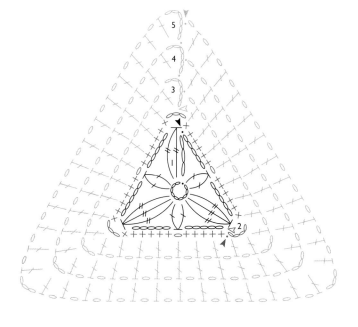

## SHAMROCK TRIANGLE
*directory view page 33*

**Skill level:** advanced
**Method of working:**
in the round

**Key:**

◯ *Chain*

• *Slip stitch*

+ *Single*

▷ *Start*

◀ *Fasten off*

## METHOD

**Special abbreviation**
**PL (picot loop):** 4 ch, ss in 3$^{rd}$ ch from hook, 5 ch, ss in 3$^{rd}$ ch from hook, 1 ch.

Make 16 ch.
**Round 1:** [1 sc, 15 ch, 1 sc, 15 ch, 1 sc] in first ch made. 3 loops.
**Round 2:** 1 ch, 23 sc in first loop, 24 sc in each of next 2 loops, ss in first ch. 72 sc.
**Round 3:** 1 ch, 1 sc in each sc, ss in first ch.
**Round 4:** Ss into each of 3 sc, 1 sc in next sc, * [PL, sk 4 sc, 1 sc in next sc] 3 times, PL, sk 8 sc, 1 sc in next sc (the 5$^{th}$ sc of next loop), * rep from * to * twice more omitting last sc of final repeat, ss in first sc of round.

**Round 5:** Ss into each of 3 sts to center of first PL, * PL, [1 sc, 5 ch, ss in 4$^{th}$ ch from hook, 1 ch, 1 sc] under 2 ch at center of next PL, [PL, 1 sc under 2 ch at center of next PL] 3 times, * rep from * to * twice more, ending in same PL as beg of round.
Fasten off.

# JONQUIL TRIANGLE
*directory view page 32*

A B C

**Skill level:** intermediate
**Method of working:**
in the round

**Key:**
⬯ *Chain*
• *Slip stitch*
+ *Single*
⩰ *2 singles in back loop*
𝈨 *Double*

𝈲 *2 doubles together*
▷ *Start/join in new color*
◀ *Fasten off*

## METHOD

**Special abbreviations**
**3-ch P (3-ch picot):** 3 ch, ss in top of last st; **5-ch P (5-ch picot):** 5 ch, ss in top of last st.

Using A, make 4 ch, join into a ring with 1 ss in first ch.
**Round 1:** 1 ch, 8 sc into ring, ss in first ch. 9 sts.
Fasten off A. Join B to back loop of any sc.
**Round 2:** 1 ch, [2 sc in back loop of next sc] 8 times, 1 sc in back loop of first sc, ss in first ch. 18 sts.
**Round 3:** 3 ch, * 2 dc tog over next 2 sc, 3-ch P, 2 ch, 1 sc in next sc, 2 ch, * rep from * to * 7 more times, 2 dc tog over next 2 sc, 3-ch P, 2 ch, ss in first of 3 ch. 6 petals.
Fasten off B. Join C to 3-ch P at top of any petal.
**Round 4:** 6 ch, 1 dc in same 3-ch P, * 3 ch, 1 dc in sc between petals, 3 ch, 1 sc in next 3-ch P, 3 ch, 1 dc in sc between petals, 3 ch, # [1 dc, 3 ch, 1 dc] in next 3-ch P, * rep from * to * once more, then once again from * to #, ss in 3rd of 6 ch.

**Round 5:** Ss into 3-ch sp, 5 ch, 2 dc in same ch sp, * 1 ch, 5 dc in next dc, 1 ch, 1 sc in next sc, 1 ch, 5 dc in next dc, 1 ch, # [2 dc, 2 ch, 2 dc] in 3-ch sp at corner, * rep from * to * once more, then once again from * to #, 1 dc in first ch sp, ss in 3rd of 5 ch.
**Round 6:** Ss into 2-ch sp, 8 ch, ss in 6th ch from hook, 3 dc in same ch sp, * [3 dc, 3-ch P, 2 dc] in next 1-ch sp, [3 dc, 3-ch P, 2 dc] in next sc, [3 dc, 3-ch P, 2 dc] in next 1-ch sp, # [4 dc, 5-ch P, 3 dc] in 2-ch sp at corner, * rep from * to * once more, then once again from * to #, 3 dc in first ch sp, ss in 3rd of 8 ch.
Fasten off C.

Blocks may be joined using the joining with picots method, page 21.

**9** **LILY TRIANGLE**
*directory view page 36*

A  B  C

**Skill level:** advanced
**Method of working:** in the round

**Key:**

| | | | |
|---|---|---|---|
| Ω | Fingerwrap | ⊤ (Treble) | Treble |
| ◯ | Chain | | 4 trebles together |
| • | Slip stitch | | |
| + | Single | | Double treble |
| ⊤ | Half double | | 5 double trebles together |
| ⊥ | Double | ▷ | Start/join in new color |
| | | ◀ | Fasten off |

## METHOD

Using A, make a fingerwrap.
**Round 1:** 3 ch, [1 hdc into wrap, 3 ch, ss in top of hdc, 1 ch] 5 times, ss in 2$^{nd}$ of 3 ch, 3 ch, ss in same place. 6 stamens.
Fasten off A. Join B to fingerwrap between any 2 hdc.
**Round 2:** Work behind round 1: 3 ch, [1 hdc over 1 ch and into wrap, 1 ch] 5 times, ss in 2$^{nd}$ of 3 ch.
**Round 3:** 3 ch, 2 dc in 1-ch sp, [1 dc in next hdc, 3 dc in next 1-ch sp, 1 dc in next hdc, 2 dc in next 1-ch sp] twice, 1 dc in next hdc, 3 dc in next 1-ch sp, ss in 2$^{nd}$ of 3 ch. 21 dc.
**Round 4:** 3 ch, 3 tr tog over next 3 dc, * 7 ch, 5 dtr tog over [same place as last insertion and foll 4 dc], 7 ch, # 4 tr tog over [same place as last insertion and foll 3 dc], * rep from * to * once more, then once again from * to #, ss in top of 3 tr tog. 6 petals: 3 large, 3 small.
Fasten off B. Join C to ch closing any 5 dtr tog (top of large petal).

**Round 5:** 3 ch, 1 sc in same place, * 8 sc in 7-ch sp, 1 sc in 4 tr tog, 8 sc in 7-ch sp, # [1 sc, 2 ch, 1 sc] in 5 dtr tog, * rep from * to * once more, then once again from * to #, ss in first of 3 ch.
**Round 6:** Ss into 2-ch sp, 7 ch, 2 tr in same ch sp, * 7 ch, sk 6 sc, 1 sc in next sc, 5 ch, sk 5 sc, 1 sc in next sc, 7 ch, sk 6 sc, # [2 tr; 3 ch, 2 tr] in next 2-ch sp, * rep from * to * once more, then once again from * to #, 1 tr in first ch sp, ss in 4$^{th}$ of 7 ch.
**Round 7:** Ss into 3-ch sp, 7 ch, 2 tr in same ch sp, * 5 ch, 3 sc in 7-ch sp, 1 sc in next sc, 5 sc in 5-ch sp, 1 sc in next sc, 3 sc in 7-ch sp, 5 ch, # [2 tr; 3 ch, 2 tr] in next 3-ch sp, * rep from * to * once more, then once again from * to #, 1 tr in first ch sp, ss in 4$^{th}$ of 7 ch.
Fasten off C.

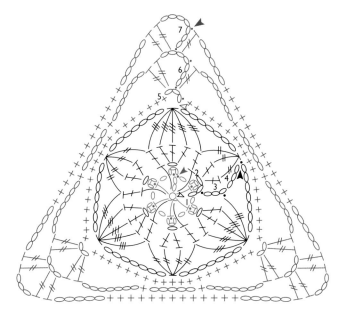

# 10 VIOLET TRIANGLE
*directory view page 35*

A B C

**Skill level:** intermediate
**Method of working:**
in the round

**Key:**
⌒ *Chain*
• *Slip stitch*
+ *Single*
† *Double*
Ŧ *Treble*
Ⅎ *Triple treble*
▷ *Start/join in new color*
◄ *Fasten off*
Ⓛ *Leaf*

## METHOD

**Special abbreviation**
**LF (leaf):** 2 tr tr tog into back loop of ss between 2 petals, 5 ch, ss into top of 2 tr tr tog just made.

Using A, make 5 ch, join into a ring with ss in first ch.
**Round 1:** [3 ch, 1 tr into ring, 3 ch, ss in top of tr just made, 3 ch, ss into ring] 4 times, 2 ch, [1 dc, 2 tr] into ring, 3 ch, ss in top of tr just made, [1 tr, 1 dc] into ring, 2 ch, ss into ring.
Fasten off A. Join B to 3-ch picot at top of large petal.
**Round 2:** 8 ch, LF, 5 ch, [1 sc into 3-ch picot at tip of next petal, 4 ch] twice, LF, [4 ch, 1 sc into next picot] twice, 5 ch, LF, 7 ch, ss into first of 8 ch.
**Round 3:** 1 ch, 7 sc into 7-ch sp, [1 sc, 3 ch, 1 sc] in 3-ch picot at tip of leaf, 5 sc in 5-ch sp, [1 sc in next sc, 4 sc in 4-ch sp] twice, [1 sc, 3 ch, 1 sc] in next picot, [4 sc in 4-ch sp, 1 sc in next sc] twice, 5 sc in 5-ch sp, [1 sc, 3 ch, 1 sc] in next picot, 7 sc in 7-ch sp, ss in first ch. 17 sc on each side.
Fasten off B. Join C to any 3-ch sp.

**Round 4:** 8 ch, 2 dc in same sp, * 1 dc in each of 17 sc, [2 dc, 5 ch, 2 dc] in 3-ch sp, * rep from * to * once more, 1 dc in each of 17 sc, 1 dc in first ch sp, ss in 3rd of 8 ch. 21 dc on each side.
**Round 5:** Ss into 5-ch sp, 6 ch, 2 dc in same ch sp, * 1 dc in each of 21 dc, [2 dc, 3 ch, 2 dc] in 5-ch sp, * rep from * to * once more, 1 dc in each of 21 dc, 1 dc in first ch sp, ss in 3rd of 6 ch. 25 dc on each side.
Fasten off C.

## 11 STONECROP TRIANGLE
*directory view page 51*

**Skill level:** advanced
**Method of working:** in the round

**Key:**

| | |
|---|---|
| ◯ | *Fingerwrap* |
| ◠ | *Chain* |
| • | *Slip stitch* |
| ⊤ | *Double* |
| ⩙ | *2 trebles together* |
| ⩘ | *3 trebles together* |
| ⩙ | *5 trebles together* |
| ◄ | *Fasten off* |

## METHOD

### Special abbreviations

**3-ch P (3-ch picot):** 3 ch, ss in 3<sup>rd</sup> ch from hook

**PL (picot loop):** [1 dc, 1 ch, 3-ch P, 1 ch, 1 dc] worked in position given.

Make a fingerwrap.

**Round 1:** 3 ch, 2 tr tog into wrap, [5 ch, 3 tr tog into wrap, 3 ch, 3 tr tog into wrap] twice, 5 ch, 3 tr tog into wrap, 3 ch, ss in top of 2 tr tog. 6 petals.

Pull gently on the starting tail to tighten the center of the flower.

**Round 2:** Ss back into previous 3-ch sp, 6 ch, * 4 ch, 5 tr tog as follows: [2 tr in 4<sup>th</sup> ch from hook, tog with 3 tr in 3<sup>rd</sup> of next 5 ch], 4 ch, 2 tr tog in 4<sup>th</sup> ch from hook (= ch closing 5 tr tog), 3 ch, # PL in 3-ch sp, 3 ch, * rep from * to * once more, then once again from * to #, 1 dc in 3-ch sp, 1 ch, 3-ch P, 1 ch, ss in 3<sup>rd</sup> of 6 ch.

**Round 3:** Ss in each of next 3 ch, 6 ch, * [3 tr tog, 9 ch, 3 tr tog] in ch closing 5 tr tog, 3 ch, PL in next 3-ch sp, 3 ch, sk 1 PL, # PL in next 3-ch sp, * rep from * to * once more, then once again from * to #, 1 dc in next 3-ch sp, 1 ch, 3-ch P, 1 ch, ss in 3<sup>rd</sup> of 6 ch.

**Round 4:** Ss in each of next 3 ch, 6 ch, * [PL, 6 ch, ss in 5<sup>th</sup> ch from hook, 1 ch, PL] in 9-ch sp, 3 ch, sk 3 tr tog, PL in next 3-ch sp, # [3 ch, sk 1 PL, PL in next 3-ch sp,] twice, 3 ch, sk 3 tr tog, * rep from * to * once more, then once again from * to #, 3 ch, sk 1 PL, PL in next 3-ch sp, 3 ch, sk 1 PL, 1 dc in first ch sp, 1 ch, 3-ch P, 1 ch, ss in 3<sup>rd</sup> of 6 ch. Fasten off.

Blocks may be joined using the joining with picots method, page 21.

# 12 MICHAELMAS DAISY TRIANGLE
*directory view page 41*

A B

**Skill level:** easy
**Method of working:**
in the round

**Key:**

⌒ *Chain*

• *Slip stitch*

+ *Single*

T *Half double*

▷ *Start/join in new color*

◄ *Fasten off*

## METHOD

### FIRST DAISY

Using A, make 5 ch, join into a ring with ss in first ch.

**Round 1:** 1 ch, 8 sc into ring, ss in first ch. 9 sts.
Fasten off A. Join B to any sc.

**Round 2:** 10 ch, ss in second of these 10 ch, * 1 sc in next sc, 9 ch, ss in first of these 9 ch, * rep from * to * 7 more times, fasten off with ss in first ch of round. 9 petals.

### SECOND DAISY

Work as for first daisy to last 2 petals of round 2.

**To join petals:** * 1 sc in next sc, 4 ch, inserting hook from back ss in any petal of first flower, 4 ch, ss in first ch of this petal, * rep from * to * once more, inserting hook in next petal of first flower to work the joining ss. Fasten off as round 2 above.

### THIRD DAISY

Work as for first daisy to last 4 petals of round 2.
Join next 2 petals to first daisy and last 2 petals to 2^nd daisy in same way as above, to match the arrangement shown on the chart.

### BORDER

Join A to 3^rd of 5 unattached petals of any daisy.

**Round 3:** 4 ch, 1 sc in next petal, 3 ch, 1 sc in next petal, * 2 ch, 1 hdc in join between next 2 petals, 2 ch, # [1 sc in next petal, 3 ch] 4 times, * rep from * to * once more, then once again from * to #, [1 sc in next petal, 3 ch] twice, ss in first of 4 ch.

**Round 4:** 3 ch, 1 sc in same ch, * [3 sc in 3-ch sp, 1 sc in next sc] twice, 2 sc in 2-ch sp, 1 sc in hdc, 2 sc in 2-ch sp, [1 sc in next sc, 3 sc in 3-ch sp] twice, # [1 sc, 2 ch, 1 sc] in next sc, * rep from * to * once more, then once again from * to #, ss in first of 3 ch. 23 sc on each side.

**Round 5:** Ss into 2-ch sp, 3 ch, 1 sc in same ch sp, * 1 sc in each of 23 sc, [1 sc, 2 ch, 1 sc] in 2-ch sp, * rep from * to * once more, 1 sc in each of 23 sc, ss in first of 3 ch. 25 sc on each side.
Fasten off A.

## 13 FLORETTE TRIANGLE
*directory view page 43*

**Skill level:** intermediate
**Method of working:** in the round

**Key:**
- ⌒ Chain
- • Slip stitch
- + Single
- ⤬ 2 singles together
- ◯ 2 half doubles together
- ⊤ Double
- ⬙ 2 doubles together
- ◀ Fasten off

## METHOD

**Special abbreviations**
**dc gp (double group):** [2 dc tog, 1 ch, 1 dc, 1 ch, 2 dc tog] all worked in same place.
**hdc gp (half-double group):** [2 hdc tog, 1 ch, 2 hdc tog, 1 ch, 2 hdc tog] all worked in same place.

Make 4 ch, join into a ring with ss in first ch.

**Round 1:** 4 ch, [3 sc into ring, 3 ch] twice, 2 sc into ring, ss in first of 4 ch. 3 sc on each side.

**Round 2:** Ss into 3-ch sp, 4 ch, 2 sc in same 3-ch sp, * 1 sc in each of 3 sc, [2 sc, 3 ch, 2 sc] in 3-ch sp, * rep from * to * once more, 1 sc in each of 3 sc, 1 sc in first ch sp, ss in first of 4 ch. 7 sc on each side.

**Round 3:** Ss into 3-ch sp, 4 ch, 2 sc in same 3-ch sp, * 1 sc in each of 7 sc, [2 sc, 3 ch, 2 sc] in 3-ch sp, * rep from * to * once more, 1 sc in each of 7 sc, 1 sc in first ch sp, ss in first of 4 ch. 11 sc on each side.

**Round 4:** Ss into 3-ch sp, 6 ch, 1 dc gp in same 3-ch sp, * 1 ch, sk 5 sc, 1 dc gp in next sc, 1 ch, sk 5 sc, # [1 dc gp, 3 ch, 1 dc gp] in 3-ch sp, * rep from * to * once more, then once again from * to #, [2 dc tog, 1 ch, 1 dc, 1 ch, 1 dc] in first ch sp, ss in 3rd of 6 ch.

**Round 5:** Ss into 3-ch sp, 6 ch, 2 dc in same 3-ch sp, * 1 ch, [1 hdc gp in central dc of next dc gp, 1 ch] 3 times, # [2 dc, 3 ch, 2 dc] in 3-ch sp, * rep from * to * once more, then once again from * to #, 1 dc in first ch sp, ss in 3rd of 6 ch.

**Round 6:** Ss into 3-ch sp, 6 ch, 2 dc in same 3-ch sp, * [4 ch, 2 sc tog over two 1-ch sps of next hdc gp] 3 times, 4 ch, # [2 dc, 3 ch, 2 dc] in next 3-ch sp, * rep from * to * once more, then once again from * to #, 1 dc in first ch sp, ss in 3rd of 6 ch.

**Round 7:** Ss into 3-ch sp, 4 ch, 1 sc in same 3-ch sp, * 1 sc in each of 2 dc, [4 sc in 4-ch sp, 1 sc in next st] 3 times, 4 sc in 4-ch sp, 1 sc in each of 2 dc, # [1 sc, 3 ch, 1 sc] in 3-ch sp, * rep from * to * once more, then once again from * to #, ss in first of 4 ch. 25 sc on each side.

Fasten off.

# 14 GRANNY ROSE SQUARE
*directory view page 43*

A B C

**Skill level:** easy
**Method of working:**
in the round

**Key:**
◯ *Chain*
• *Slip stitch*
+ *Single*
⌇ *Treble*

⌇ *Double in sc of round below*
▷ *Start/join in new color*
◀ *Fasten off*

## METHOD

Using A, make 6 ch, join into a ring with ss in first ch.

**Round 1:** 6 ch, [5 tr into ring, 2 ch] 3 times, 4 tr into ring, ss in 4th of 6 ch.

**Round 2:** Ss into 2-ch sp, 7 ch, [1 sc in next 2-ch sp, 6 ch] 3 times, ss in first of 7 ch.

**Round 3:** Ss into 6-ch sp, 4 ch, [4 tr; 2 ch, 5 tr] in same ch sp, * [5 tr; 2 ch, 5 tr] into next 6-ch sp, * rep from * to * twice more, ss in 4th of 4 ch.

Fasten off A. Join B to any 2-ch sp.

**Round 4:** 6 ch, 5 tr in same ch sp, * 1 tr in space between next 2 groups, 3 dc in sc of round 2 below, 1 tr in same space between 2 groups, [5 tr; 2 ch, 5 tr] in next 2-ch sp, * rep from * to * twice more, 1 tr in space between next 2 groups, 3 dc in sc of round 2 below, 1 tr in same space between 2 groups, 4 tr in same 2-ch sp as beg of round, ss in 4th of 6 ch.

Fasten off B. Join C to any 2-ch sp.

**Round 5:** 6 ch, 5 tr in same ch sp, * [5 tr in space between next 2 groups] twice, [5 tr; 2 ch, 5 tr] in next 2-ch sp, * rep from * to * twice more, [5 tr in space between next 2 groups] twice, 4 tr in same 2-ch sp as beg of round, ss in 4th of 6 ch.

**Round 6:** Ss into 2-ch sp, 6 ch, 5 tr in same ch sp, * [5 tr in space between next 2 groups] 3 times, [5 tr; 2 ch, 5 tr] in next 2-ch sp, * rep from * to * twice more, [5 tr in space between next 2 groups] 3 times, 4 tr in same 2-ch sp as beg of round, ss in 4th of 6 ch. 25 tr on each side of square.

Fasten off C.

## 15 STAR FLOWER SQUARE
*directory view page 39*

● ● ●
A B C

**Skill level:** intermediate
**Method of working:** in the round

**Key:**
⌒ *Chain*
· *Slip stitch*
+ *Single*
 *3 trebles together*

 *4 double trebles together*
▷ *Start/join in new color*
◀ *Fasten off*

---

## METHOD

Using A, make 12 ch, join into a ring with ss in first ch.
**Round 1:** 1 ch, 23 sc into ring, ss in first ch. 24 sc.
**Round 2:** 6 ch, 3 dtr tog over next 3 sc, * 7 ch, 4 dtr tog over [same sc and next 3 sc], * rep from * to * 6 more times, ending with last insertion in base of 6 ch, 7 ch, ss in st closing first petal. 8 petals. Fasten off A. Join B to st closing any petal.
**Round 3:** 1 ch, * 7 sc in 7-ch sp, 1 sc in st closing next petal, * rep from * to * 7 more times omitting last sc, ss in first ch. 64 sc.
**Round 4:** 1 ch, * 3 ch, sk 1 sc, 1 sc in next sc, * rep from * to * all around omitting last sc, ss in first ch. 32 ch sps.
**Round 5:** Ss into next 2 ch, 1 ch, * 3 ch, 1 sc in next 3-ch sp, * rep from * to * all around omitting last sc, ss in first ch.
**Round 6:** As round 5. Fasten off B. Join C to next 3-ch sp.
**Round 7:** 1 ch, * [3 sc in next 3-ch sp] 3 times, 1 sc in next 3-ch sp, 3 ch, sk 1 ch sp, [3 tr tog, 5 ch, 4 dtr tog, 3 ch, ss in top of 4 dtr tog, 5 ch, 3 tr tog] all in next 3-ch sp, 3 ch, sk 1 ch sp, 1 sc in next ch sp, * rep from * to * 3 more times omitting last sc, ss in first ch. Fasten off C.

### MIX AND MATCH: 15 + 16

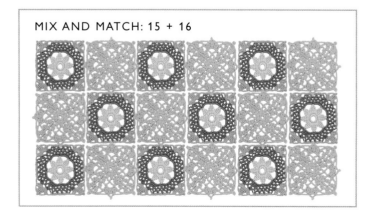

**CORAL TRELLIS SQUARE**
*directory view page 46*

**Skill level:** intermediate
**Method of working:** in the round

**Key:**

- ⌒  *Chain*
- •  *Slip stitch*
- +  *Single*
- ⬧  *Cluster*
- ⫟  *Double treble*
- ◀  *Fasten off*

## METHOD

**Special abbreviation**

**CL (cluster):** yrh twice, insert as directed, [yrh, pull through 2 loops] twice (2 loops remain on hook), * yrh, insert under 2 threads of lowest step of st just made, [yrh, pull through 2 loops] twice, * rep from * to * once more, yrh, pull through all 4 loops on hook.

Make 8 ch, join into a ring with ss in first ch.

**Round 1:** 7 ch, [CL into ring, 5 ch, CL into ring, 2 ch, 1 dtr into ring, 2 ch] 3 times, CL into ring, 5 ch, CL into ring, 2 ch, ss in 5th of 7 ch.

**Round 2:** 7 ch, [CL in 2-ch sp, 5 ch, 1 sc in 5-ch sp, 5 ch, CL in 2-ch sp, 2 ch, 1 dtr in dtr, 2 ch] 3 times, CL in 2-ch sp, 5 ch, 1 sc in 5-ch sp, 5 ch, CL in 2-ch sp, 2 ch, ss in 5th of 7 ch.

**Round 3:** 7 ch, * CL in 2-ch sp, [5 ch, 1 sc in 5-ch sp] twice, 5 ch, CL in 2-ch sp, 2 ch, # 1 dtr in dtr; 2 ch, * rep from * to * twice more, then once again from * to #, ss in 5th of 7 ch.

**Round 4:** 7 ch, * CL in 2-ch sp, 5 ch, 1 sc in 5-ch sp, [1 ch, CL] 3 times in next 5-ch sp, 1 ch, 1 sc in next 5-ch sp, 5 ch, CL in 2-ch sp, 2 ch, # 1 dtr in dtr, 2 ch, * rep from * to * twice more, then once again from * to #, ss in 5th of 7 ch.

**Round 5:** 6 ch, ss in 5th ch from hook, * 5 ch, 1 sc in next 5-ch sp, 5 ch, 1 sc in 1-ch sp between 1st and 2nd of 3 CL, 6 ch, ss in 4th ch from hook, 2 ch, 1 sc in 1-ch sp between 2nd and 3rd of same 3 CL, 5 ch, 1 sc in next 5-ch sp, 5 ch, # 1 sc in dtr, 5 ch, ss in top of sc, * rep from * to * twice more, then once again from * to #, ss in first of 6 ch.
Fasten off.

Blocks may be joined using the joining with picots method, page 21.

**BLOSSOM SQUARE**
*directory view page 36*

A  B

**Skill level:** intermediate
**Method of working:**
in the round

**Key:**
⌒ *Chain*
• *Slip stitch*
⊤ *Double*

⬭ *Puff stitch of 3 half doubles together*
▷ *Join in new color*
◀ *Fasten off*

## METHOD

**Special abbreviations**
**5-ch P (5-ch picot):** 5 ch, ss in first of these 5 ch.
**PS (puff stitch):** 3 hdc tog in same place.

Using A, make 5 ch, join into a ring with ss in first ch.
**Round 1:** 2 ch, 2 hdc tog into ring, 5-ch P, [4 ch, PS into ring, 5-ch P] 3 times, 4 ch, ss into first 5-ch P made.
**Round 2:** 2 ch, [2 hdc tog, 5-ch P, 4 ch, PS] in first 5-ch P, * 5-ch P, [PS, 4 ch, PS, 5-ch P, 4 ch, PS] in next 5-ch P, * rep * to * twice more, 5-ch P, PS in same 5-ch P as beg of round, 4 ch, ss in first 5-ch P of round.
**Round 3:** 2 ch, [2 hdc tog, 5-ch P, 4 ch, PS] in first 5-ch P, * 5-ch P, [PS, 4 ch, PS, 5-ch P] in next 5-ch P, [PS, 4 ch, PS, 5-ch P, 4 ch, PS] in corner 5-ch P, * rep * to * ending PS in same 5-ch P as beg of round, 4 ch, ss in first 5-ch P of this round.

**Round 4:** 2 ch, [2 hdc tog, 5-ch P, 4 ch, PS] in first 5-ch P, * 5-ch P, [PS, 4 ch, PS, 5-ch P] in each of next two 5-ch P, [PS, 4 ch, PS, 5-ch P, 4 ch, PS] in corner 5-ch P, * rep * to * ending PS in same 5-ch P as beg of round, 4 ch, ss in first 5-ch P of round.
Fasten off A. Join B to any corner 5-ch P.
**Round 5:** 6 ch, 3 dc in same 5-ch P, * [5 dc in next 5-ch P] 3 times, [3 dc, 3 ch, 3 dc] in corner 5-ch P, * rep from * to * ending 2 dc in same 5-ch P as beg of round, ss in 3rd of 6 ch.
**Round 6:** Ss in each of next 2 ch, 6 ch, 2 dc in 3-ch sp, * 1 dc in each of 21 dc, [2 dc, 3 ch, 2 dc] in 3-ch sp, * rep from * to * ending 1 dc in same 3-ch sp as beg of round, ss in 3rd of 6 ch. 25 dc on each side.
Fasten off B.

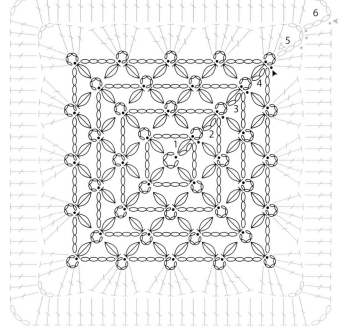

# 18 BUTTERFLY SQUARE
*directory view page 40*

**Skill level:** advanced
**Method of working:** in the round

**Key:**

⌒ Chain
• Slip stitch
+ Single
⋏ Single in back loop
⊤ Half double
⨑ Double
⨑ Treble
⨑ Double treble
▷ Start/join in new color
◄ Fasten off
↵ Direction of working

## METHOD

**Round 1:** Using A, 13 ch, ss in 13<sup>th</sup> ch from hook, 12 ch, ss in 9<sup>th</sup> ch from hook, 9 ch, ss in 9<sup>th</sup> ch from hook, ss in each of next 3 ch, 13 ch, ss in 13<sup>th</sup> ch from hook. 4 loops made for wings: 1 large, 2 small, 1 large.

**Round 2:** 1 ch, [1 sc, 2 hdc, 3 dc, 3 tr; 1 ch, 1 dtr; 1 ch, 3 tr, 3 dc, 2 hdc, 1 sc] in 13-ch loop, sk 1 ch, ss in next ch, sk 1 ch, [1 sc, 2 hdc, 2 dc, 2 tr; 1 ch, 1 dtr; 1 ch, 2 tr, 2 dc, 2 hdc, 1 sc] in 9-ch loop, 1 sc in base of body, work 17 sts as before in 9-ch loop, sk 1 ss, ss in next ss, sk 1 ss, work 21 sts as before in 13-ch loop, ss in first ch of round.

**Round 3:** 3 ch, sk [1 sc, 1 hdc], ss in next hdc, * [1 ch, ss in next st] 6 times, 1 ch, sk 1 ch, [1 sc, 3 hdc, 1 sc] in dtr; 1 ch, sk 1 ch, [ss in next st, 1 ch] 6 times, # ss in next st, sk [1 hdc, 1 sc, 1 ss, 1 sc, 1 hdc], ss in next st, [1 ch, ss in next st] 4 times, 1 ch, sk 1 ch, [1 sc, 3 hdc, 1 sc] in dtr; 1 ch, sk 1 ch, [ss in next st, 1 ch] 4 times, * rep from * to * once more, ss in next st, sk [1 hdc, 1 sc, 1 ss, 1 sc, 1 hdc], ss in next st, rep from * to # once more, ss in next st, ss in 3<sup>rd</sup> of 3 ch at beg of round.
Fasten off A. Join B to 3-ch sp at tip of top right wing.

**Round 4:** 5 ch, 1 dc in same ch sp, 5 ch, sk 5 sts, 1 sc in bl (back loop) of next ch, 5 ch, sk 9 sts, 2 dc tog inserting hook at either side of 3 ch at beg of round 3,

5 ch, sk 9 sts, 1 sc in bl of next ch, 5 ch, sk 5 sts, [1 dc, 2 ch, 1 dc] in 3-ch sp at tip of 2<sup>nd</sup> wing, * 5 ch, sk 5 sts, 1 sc in bl of next ch, 5 ch, 1 tr in sp between wings, 5 ch, * sk 5 sts, 1 sc in bl of next ch, 5 ch, sk 5 sts, [1 dc, 2 ch, 1 dc] in 3-ch sp at tip of 3<sup>rd</sup> wing, 5 ch, sk 4 sts, 1 sc in bl of next sc, 5 ch, 1 tr in sp between wings, 5 ch, sk 5 sts, 1 sc in bl of next sc, 5 ch, sk 4 sts, [1 dc, 2 ch, 1 dc] in 3-ch sp at tip of 4<sup>th</sup> wing, rep from * to * once more, sk 9 sts, 1 sc in bl of next ch, 5 ch, sk 5 sts, ss in 3<sup>rd</sup> of 5 ch at beg of round.

**Round 5:** Ss into 2-ch sp, 5 ch, 1 dc in same ch sp, * [5 ch, 1 sc in next ch sp] 4 times, 5 ch, [1 dc, 2 ch, 1 dc] in 2-ch sp at wingtip, 5 ch, 1 sc in next ch sp, [5 ch, 1 dc in next ch sp] 3 times, 5 ch, [1 dc, 2 ch, 1 dc] in 2-ch sp, [5 ch, 1 dc in next ch sp] 4 times, 5 ch, [1 dc, 2 ch, 1 dc] in 2-ch sp, [5 ch, 1 dc in next ch sp] 3 times, 5 ch, 1 sc in next ch sp, 5 ch, ss in 3<sup>rd</sup> of 3 ch at beg of round. 5 ch sps on each side.

**Round 6:** Ss into 2-ch sp, 8 ch, 2 dc in same ch sp, * 3 ch, 1 sc in next ch sp, 5 ch, 1 sc in next ch sp, [3 dc, 3 ch, 3 dc] in next ch sp, 1 sc in next ch sp, 5 ch, 1 sc in next ch sp, 3 ch, # [2 dc, 5 ch, 2 dc] in 2-ch sp at corner, * rep from * to * twice more, then once again from * to #, 1 dc in first ch sp, ss in 3<sup>rd</sup> of 8 ch. Fasten off B.

## 19 THREE DAISY SQUARE
*directory view page 39*

A  B

**Skill level:** easy
**Method of working:**
in rows and in the round

**Key:**

⌒ *Chain*

• *Slip stitch*

+ *Single*

† *Double*

↩ *Direction of working*

▷ *Join in new color*

◀ *Fasten off*

## METHOD

**SQUARE**
Using A, make 30 ch.
**Row 1:** 1 dc in 4th ch from hook,
1 dc in each of 26 ch. 28 dc.
**Row 2:** 3 ch, sk first dc, 1 dc in
each rem dc, 1 dc in 3rd of 3 ch.
**Row 3:** 3 ch, sk first dc, 1 dc in
each of 21 dc, 2 ch, sk 2 dc, 1 dc in
each of 3 dc, 1 dc in 3rd of 3 ch.
**Row 4:** As row 2, working 2 dc
into 2-ch sp.
**Rows 5–6:** As row 2.
**Row 7:** 3 ch, sk first dc, 1 dc in
each of 12 dc, 2 ch, sk 2 dc, 1 dc in
each of 12 dc, 1 dc in 3rd of 3 ch.
**Row 8:** As row 2, working 2 dc
into 2-ch sp.
**Rows 9–10:** As row 2.
**Row 11:** 3 ch, sk first dc, 1 dc in
each of 3 dc, 2 ch, sk 2 dc, 1 dc in
each of 21 dc, 1 dc in 3rd of 3 ch.

**Row 12:** As row 2, working 2 dc
into 2-ch sp.
**Row 13:** As row 2.
Fasten off A.

**DAISIES**
Work first daisy in the round
around a hole.
**Round 1:** With RS facing, join B to
first of 2 skipped dc on row 2, 1 ch,
1 sc in next dc, 1 sc in corner, 2 sc
in dc at left edge of hole, 1 sc in
corner, 1 sc in base of each of 2 dc
at top of hole, 1 sc in corner, 2 sc
in dc at right edge of hole, 1 sc in
corner, ss in first ch. 12 sts.
**Round 2:** 6 ch, [ss in next sc, 6 ch]
11 times, ss in last ss of round 1.
Fasten off B.
Make 2 more daisies in the same
way, around the rem holes.

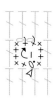

**MIX AND MATCH: 19 + 20**

## 20 EMBOSSED FLOWER SQUARE
*directory view page 41*

**Skill level:** easy
**Method of working:** in rows

**Key:**
- ⌒ Chain
- • Slip stitch
- ┬ Double
- ◄ Fasten off
- ✳ Start of flower
- ↵ Direction of working
- 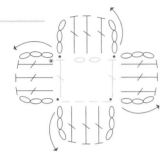 Flower worked around hole

## METHOD

Make 30 ch.
**Row 1 (WS):** 1 dc in 3$^{rd}$ ch from hook, 1 dc in each of 26 ch. 28 dc.
**Row 2:** 3 ch, sk first dc, 1 dc in each of 3 dc, * 2 ch, sk 2 dc, 1 dc in each of 4 dc, * rep from * to * twice more, 2 ch, sk 2 dc, 1 dc in each of 3 dc, 1 dc in 3$^{rd}$ of 3 ch.
**Row 3:** 3 ch, sk first dc, 1 dc in each of 3 dc, * 2 dc in 2-ch sp, 1 dc in next dc, 2 ch, sk 2 dc, 1 dc in next dc, make flower around edge of mesh space just made:
Working counter-clockwise and always inserting the hook from inside the mesh space (as if it were a foundation ring), 3 ch, 3 dc under stem of last dc made (at left side of space), 3 ch, ss into corner (that is, top of dc of previous row) 3 ch, 1 dc in same place, 1 dc in top of each of next 2 dc of previous row, 3 ch, ss into corner, 3 ch, 3 dc under next dc (at right side of space), 3 ch, ss into corner, 3 ch, 3 dc under 2 ch (across top of space), 3 ch, then inserting hook from the front ss into top of next dc of main row. 4 petals made. Hold the first petal made to the front and work 2 dc into next 2-ch sp of previous row, * 1 dc in next dc, 2 ch, sk 2 dc, 1 dc in next dc, rep from * to * once more, 1 dc in each of 3 dc, 1 dc in 3$^{rd}$ of 3 ch.

**Row 4:** When working into 2-ch sps, part the petal sts to work the dc between them, over the enclosed ch: 3 ch, sk first dc, 1 dc in each of 3 dc, * 2 ch, sk 2 dc, 1 dc in next dc, 2 dc in 2-ch sp, 1 dc in next dc, * rep from * to * twice more, 2 ch, sk 2 dc, 1 dc in each of 3 dc, 1 dc in 3$^{rd}$ of 3 ch.
**Row 5:** As row 1.
**Row 6:** 3 ch, sk first dc, 1 dc in each of 3 dc, * 2 ch, sk 2 dc, 1 dc in next dc, 2 dc in 2-ch sp, 1 dc in next dc, * rep from * to * twice more, 2 ch, sk 2 dc, 1 dc in each of 3 dc, 1 dc in 3$^{rd}$ of 3 ch.
Rep rows 3–6 once more, then rows 3–4 once again. 12 rows.
**Row 13:** 3 ch, sk first dc, 1 dc in each dc and 2 dc in each 2-ch sp, ending 1 dc in 3$^{rd}$ of 3 ch.
Fasten off.

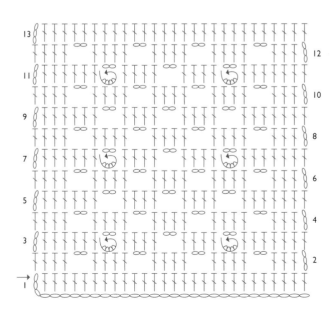

**Skill level:** easy
**Method of working:** in the round

**Key:**
⌒ *Chain*
• *Slip stitch*
+ *Single*
† *Double*
⊤ *Treble*
▷ *Start/join in new color*
◄ *Fasten off*

## METHOD

Using A, make 6 ch, join into a ring with ss in first ch.

**Round 1:** 1 ch, [3 ch, 2 tr into ring, 3 ch, 1 sc into ring] 3 times, 3 ch, 2 tr into ring, 3 ch, ss in first ch. 4 petals.

Fasten off A. Join B to sc between any 2 petals.

**Round 2:** 6 ch, 1 dc in same place, [3 ch, sk 1 petal, [1 dc, 3 ch, 1 dc] in next sc] 3 times, 3 ch, sk 1 petal, ss in 3rd of 6 ch.

**Round 3:** 3 ch, [3 dc in next 3-ch sp, 2 ch, 1 sc in next dc, 2 ch] 7 times, 3 dc in next 3-ch sp, 2 ch, ss in first of 3 ch. 8 petals.

Fasten off B. Join C to any sc before 3 dc worked into a ch sp.

**Round 4:** 8 ch, sk 1 petal, 1 sc in next sc, [5 ch, sk 1 petal, 1 sc in next sc, 7 ch, sk 1 petal, 1 sc in next sc] 3 times, 5 ch, sk 1 petal, ss in first of 8 ch. 8 loops.

**Round 5:** Ss into each of next 4 ch, 5 ch, 4 dc in same ch sp, * 1 dc in next sc, 5 dc in 5-ch sp, 1 dc in next sc, # [4 dc, 2 ch, 4 dc] in 7-ch sp, * rep from * to * twice more, then once again from * to #, 3 dc in first ch sp, ss in 3rd of 5 ch. 15 dc on each side.

**Round 6:** Ss into 2-ch sp, 5 ch, 2 dc in same place, * 1 dc in each of 15 dc, [2 dc, 2 ch, 2 dc] in 2-ch sp, * rep from * to * twice more, 1 dc in each of 15 dc, 1 dc in first ch sp, ss in 3rd of 5 ch. 19 dc on each side.

**Round 7:** Ss into 2-ch sp, 5 ch, 2 dc in same place, * 1 dc in each of 19 dc, [2 dc, 2 ch, 2 dc] in 2-ch sp, * rep from * to * twice more, 1 dc in each of 19 dc, 1 dc in first ch sp, ss in 3rd of 5 ch. 23 dc on each side.

Fasten off C. Join A to 2-ch sp at any corner.

**Round 8:** 3 ch, 1 sc in same ch sp, * 1 sc in each of 23 dc, [1 sc, 2 ch, 1 sc] in 2-ch sp, * rep from * to * twice more, 1 sc in each of 23 dc, ss in first of 3 ch. 25 sc on each side.

Fasten off A.

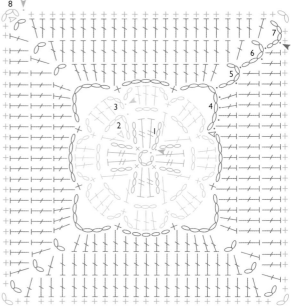

# 22 CHRYSANTHEMUM SQUARE
directory view page 51

A B C

**Skill level:** intermediate
**Method of working:** center is worked in a spiral and the outer part in the round

**Key:**
- ⌒ *Chain*
- • *Slip stitch*
- + *Single*
- ⫩ *Single in side edge of previous single*
- ⊤ *Half double*
- † *Double*
- ‡ *Treble*
- ⊕ *4 doubles together in same place*
- ▷ *Start/join in new color*
- ◀ *Fasten off*

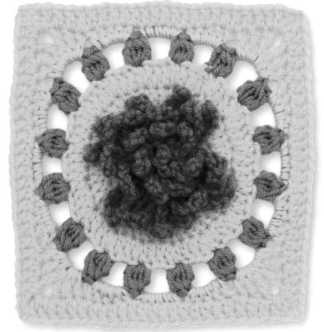

## METHOD

**Central flower:** Using A, make 6 ch, ss in 3rd ch from hook, 2 ch, sk 2 ch, 1 sc in first ch made. Do not turn.
[5 ch, ss in 3rd ch from hook, 2 ch, sk 2 ch, 1 sc in side edge of sc, do not turn] 8 times.
[7 ch, ss in 3rd ch from hook, 4 ch, sk 4 ch, 1 sc in side edge of sc, do not turn] 9 times.
[9 ch, ss in 3rd ch from hook, 6 ch, sk 6 ch, 1 sc in side edge of sc, do not turn] 9 times.
Without turning work and counting along side edge, ss in 8th sc. Fasten off A.
**Round 1:** Turn work over and join B to back loop of any sc in the ring just made, 3 ch, 2 dc in back loop of each of 7 sts, 1 dc in base of 3 ch, ss in 3rd of 3 ch. 16 dc.
**Round 2:** 3 ch, 2 dc in each dc, 1 dc in base of 3 ch, ss in 3rd of 3 ch. 32 dc.
**Round 3:** 3 ch, [1 dc in next dc, 2 dc in next dc] 15 times, 1 dc in last dc, 1 dc in base of 3 ch, ss in 3rd of 3 ch. 48 dc.
**Round 4:** 3 ch, [1 dc in each of 2 dc, 2 dc in next dc] 15 times, 1 dc in each of 2 dc, 1 dc in base of 3 ch. 64 dc. Fasten off B.

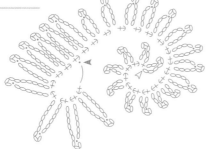

**Round 5:** Join C to any dc, 2 ch, 3 dc tog in same place as base of 2 ch, [4 ch, sk 3 dc, 4 dc tog in next dc] 15 times, 4 ch, sk 3 dc, ss in 3 dc tog. 80 sts. Fasten off C.
**Round 6:** Join B to any 4-ch sp, 6 ch, [2 tr, 1 dc] in same 4-ch sp, * [2 dc, 3 hdc] in next 4-ch sp, 5 sc in next 4-ch sp, [3 hdc, 2 dc] in next 4-ch sp, [1 dc, 2 tr, 2 ch, 2 tr, 1 dc] in next 4-ch sp, * rep from * to * 3 more times ending last rep with [1 dc, 1 tr] in first ch sp, ss in 4th of 6 ch. 21 sts on each side.
**Round 7:** Ss into 2-ch sp, 5 ch, 2 dc in same 2-ch sp, * 1 dc in each of 21 sts, [2 dc, 2 ch, 2 dc] in 2-ch sp, * rep from * to * ending last rep with 1 dc in first ch sp, ss in 3rd of 5 ch. 25 sts on each side. Fasten off B.
Coil the free end of the central flower tightly and sew it in place.

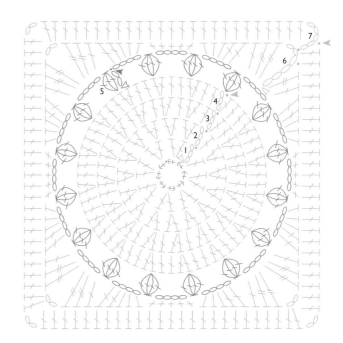

## 23 LACY DAISY SQUARE
*directory view page 34*

A  B  C

**Skill level:** easy
**Method of working:** in the round

**Key:**
- ⌒ Chain
- • Slip stitch
- + Single
- ⊤ Half double
- ⊤ Double
- ⫢ Double treble in back loop
- ▷ Start/join in new color
- ◄ Fasten off

## METHOD

Using A, make 6 ch, join into a ring with ss in first ch.

**Round 1:** 1 ch, 11 sc into ring, ss in first ch. 12 sts.
Fasten off A. Join B to back loop of any sc.

**Round 2:** 6 ch, 1 dtr in back loop of same sc, 1 ch, [1 dtr, 1 ch] twice in back loop of each sc, ss in 5$^{th}$ of 6 ch. 24 petals.
Fasten off B. Join C to any 1-ch sp.

**Round 3:** 5 ch, 1 dc in same ch sp, * 1 ch, 1 hdc in next ch sp, [1 ch, 1 sc in next ch sp] 3 times, 1 ch, 1 hdc in next ch sp, 1 ch, # [1 dc, 2 ch, 1 dc] in next ch sp, * rep from * to * twice more, then once again from * to #, ss in 3$^{rd}$ of 5 ch.

**Round 4:** * Ss in 2-ch sp, 5 ch, ss in same ch sp, 4 ch, sk [1 dc, 1 ch, 1 hdc], ss in next ch sp, 4 ch, sk [1 sc, 1 ch], ss in next sc, 4 ch, sk [1 ch, 1 sc], ss in next ch sp, 4 ch, sk [1 hdc, 1 ch, 1 dc], * rep from * to * 3 more times, ss in same 2-ch sp as beg of round.

**Round 5:** Ss in each of next 2 ch, ss under rem 3 ch, * 5 ch, ss in same ch sp, [4 ch, ss in next ch sp] 5 times, * rep from * to * 3 more times, ss in same ch sp as beg of round.

**Round 6:** Ss in each of next 2 ch, ss under rem 3 ch, * 5 ch, ss in same ch sp, [4 ch, ss in next ch sp] 6 times, * rep from * to * 3 more times, ss in same ch sp as beg of round.

**Round 7:** Ss in each of next 2 ch, ss under rem 3 ch, 6 ch, 1 dc in same ch sp, * [2 ch, 1 dc in next ch sp] 7 times, 3 ch, 1 dc in same ch sp, * rep from * to * 3 more times, [2 ch, 1 dc in next ch sp] 6 times, 2 ch, ss in 3$^{rd}$ of 6 ch.

**Round 8:** Ss in 3-ch sp, 5 ch, 1 dc in same ch sp, 3 dc in each 2-ch sp and [1 dc, 3 ch, 1 dc] in each corner sp all around, ss in 3$^{rd}$ of 5 ch. 23 dc on each side.

**Round 9:** Ss in 3-ch sp, 3 ch, 1 sc in same ch sp, 1 sc in each dc and [1 sc, 2 ch, 1 sc] in each corner sp all around, ss in 2$^{nd}$ of 3 ch. 25 sc on each side.
Fasten off C.

## 24 CROCUS SQUARE
directory view page 33

A B C

**Skill level:** intermediate
**Method of working:** diagonally in rows

**Key:**
- ⌒ Chain
- • Slip stitch
- ⊤ Double
- ⋏ 2 doubles together
- ⊥ 2 linked doubles
- 3 doubles in stitch below
- ⊤ Treble
- 2 trebles together
- [2 linked doubles, 1 double, 1 treble, 1 double, 2 linked doubles] all worked together
- ▷ Start/join in new color
- ◀ Fasten off

## METHOD

**Special abbreviation**

**2 ldc (2 linked dc):** * yrh, insert hook in same ch sp as last st and pull through a loop, * rep from * to * in next ch sp, (5 loops on hook), yrh, pull through 4 loops, yrh, pull through 2 loops.

Using A, make 59 ch.
**Row 1:** 1 dc in 4th ch from hook, 1 dc in each of 24 ch, 2 dc tog over [next and foll 4th ch], 1 dc in each of rem 26 ch. 27 sts on each of 2 sides.
**Row 2:** 3 ch, sk first dc, 1 dc in each of 23 dc, 2 dc tog over [next and foll 4th st], 1 dc in each of 23 dc, 1 dc in 3rd of 3 ch. 25 sts on each side.
**Row 3:** 3 ch, sk first dc, * sk next 2 dc, [1 dc, 1 ch, 1 dc, 1 ch, 1 dc] in next dc, sk 2 dc, 1 dc in next dc, * rep from * to * twice more, sk 2 dc, [1 dc, 1 ch, 1 dc] in next dc, 2 dc tog over [next and foll 4th st], [1 dc, 1 ch, 1 dc] in next dc, sk 2 dc, 1 dc in next dc, rep from * to * 3 times, working final dc in 3rd of 3 ch.
**Row 4:** 3 ch, sk first dc, 1 dc in each dc and ch sp to center 5 sts, 2 dc tog over [next and foll 4th st], 1 dc in each dc and ch sp ending 1 dc in 3rd of 3 ch. 21 sts on each side. Fasten off A. Join B to same place.
**Row 5:** 4 ch, sk first dc, * sk next 2 dc, [1 tr, 3 ch, ss, 3 ch, 1 tr] in next dc, sk 2 dc, 1 tr in next dc, * rep from * to *

once more, sk 2 dc, [1 tr, 3 ch, ss,] in next dc, 3 ch, 4 tr tog over [same dc, and foll 3rd, 7th, and 10th dc], 3 ch, [ss, 3 ch, 1 tr] in same place as last insertion, sk 2 dc, 1 tr in next dc, rep from * to * twice more, working final tr in 3rd of 3 ch. Fasten off B. Join C to same place.
**Row 6:** 2 ch, sk [2 tr, 3 ch], * [2 tr tog, 2 ch, 2 tr tog] in next ss, 3 ch, sk [3 ch, 3 tr, 3 ch], * rep from * to * once more, [2 tr tog, 2 ch, 2 tr tog] in next ss, sk 3 tr, rep from * to * twice more, [2 tr tog, 2 ch, 2 tr tog] in next ss, 1 ch, sk [3 ch, 1 tr], 1 sc in 4th of 4 ch. 3 flowers on each side. Fasten off C. Join A to same place.
**Row 7:** 3 ch, 1 dc in first ch sp, 2 ldc, * 1 dc in same 2-ch sp, 2 ldc, 3 dc in center tr of 3 of row 5 below, * 2 ldc, 1 dc in same 2-ch sp, 2 ldc, 3 dc in center tr of 3 of row 5 below, work foll 5 sts tog: [2 ldc, 1 dc in same ch sp, 1 tr between 2 flowers at corner, 1 dc in next ch sp and 2 ldc], 3 dc in center tr of 3 of row 5 below, 2 ldc, rep from * to * once more, 2 ldc, 1 dc in same ch sp, 2 ldc, 2 dc in last tr of row 5 below.
**Row 8:** 3 ch, sk first dc, 1 dc in each dc to center 5 sts, 2 dc tog over [next and foll 4th st], 1 dc in each dc, ending 1 dc in 3rd of 3 ch. 13 sts on each side.
**Rows 9–13:** As row 8. 3 sts on each side.
**Row 14:** 2 ch, sk 4 sts, 1 dc in 3rd of 3 ch. Fasten off A.

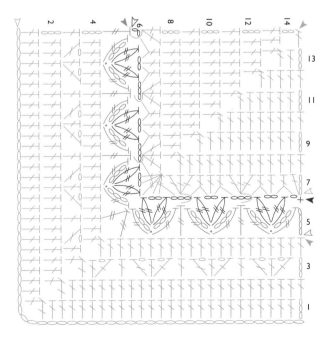

## 25 FUCHSIA SQUARE
directory view page 45

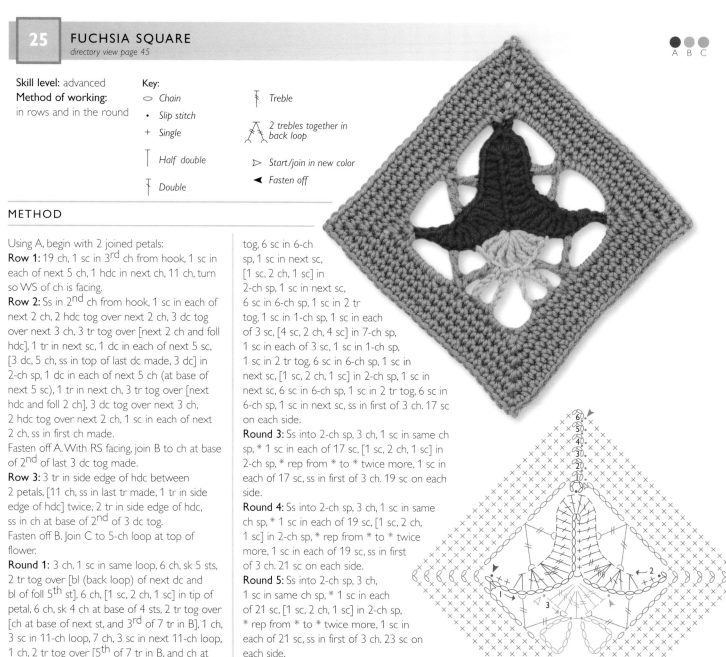

**Skill level:** advanced
**Method of working:**
in rows and in the round

**Key:**

⌒ *Chain*

• *Slip stitch*

+ *Single*

⊤ *Half double*

⊤ *Double*

⊤ *Treble*

⋀ *2 trebles together in back loop*

▷ *Start/join in new color*

◄ *Fasten off*

## METHOD

Using A, begin with 2 joined petals:

**Row 1:** 19 ch, 1 sc in 3rd ch from hook, 1 sc in each of next 5 ch, 1 hdc in next ch, 11 ch, turn so WS of ch is facing.

**Row 2:** Ss in 2nd ch from hook, 1 sc in each of next 2 ch, 2 hdc tog over next 2 ch, 3 dc tog over next 3 ch, 3 tr tog over [next 2 ch and foll hdc], 1 tr in next sc, 1 dc in each of next 5 sc, [3 dc, 5 ch, ss in top of last dc made, 3 dc] in 2-ch sp, 1 dc in each of next 5 ch (at base of next 5 sc), 1 tr in next ch, 3 tr tog over [next hdc and foll 2 ch], 3 dc tog over next 3 ch, 2 hdc tog over next 2 ch, 1 sc in each of next 2 ch, ss in first ch made.

Fasten off A. With RS facing, join B to ch at base of 2nd of last 3 dc tog made.

**Row 3:** 3 tr in side edge of hdc between 2 petals, [11 ch, ss in last tr made, 1 tr in side edge of hdc] twice, 2 tr in side edge of hdc, ss in ch at base of 2nd of 3 dc tog.

Fasten off B. Join C to 5-ch loop at top of flower.

**Round 1:** 3 ch, 1 sc in same loop, 6 ch, sk 5 sts, 2 tr tog over [bl (back loop) of next dc and bl of foll 5th st], 6 ch, [1 sc, 2 ch, 1 sc] in tip of petal, 6 ch, sk 4 ch at base of 4 sts, 2 tr tog over [ch at base of next st, and 3rd of 7 tr in B], 1 ch, 3 sc in 11-ch loop, 7 ch, 3 sc in next 11-ch loop, 1 ch, 2 tr tog over [5th of 7 tr in B, and ch at base of foll 5th st], 6 ch, sk ch at base of 4 sts, [1 sc, 2 ch, 1 sc] in tip of petal, 6 ch, sk 4 sts, 2 tr tog over [bl of next st and bl of foll 5th st], 6 ch, sk 5 sts, ss in first of 3 ch.

**Round 2:** Ss into 2-ch sp, 3 ch, 1 sc in same ch sp, 1 sc in next sc, 6 sc in 6-ch sp, 1 sc in 2 tr tog, 6 sc in 6-ch sp, 1 sc in next sc, [1 sc, 2 ch, 1 sc] in 2-ch sp, 1 sc in next sc, 6 sc in 6-ch sp, 1 sc in 2 tr tog, 1 sc in 1-ch sp, 1 sc in each of 3 sc, [4 sc, 2 ch, 4 sc] in 7-ch sp, 1 sc in each of 3 sc, 1 sc in 1-ch sp, 1 sc in 2 tr tog, 6 sc in 6-ch sp, 1 sc in next sc, [1 sc, 2 ch, 1 sc] in 2-ch sp, 1 sc in next sc, 6 sc in 6-ch sp, 1 sc in 2 tr tog, 6 sc in 6-ch sp, 1 sc in next sc, ss in first of 3 ch. 17 sc on each side.

**Round 3:** Ss into 2-ch sp, 3 ch, 1 sc in same ch sp, * 1 sc in each of 17 sc, [1 sc, 2 ch, 1 sc] in 2-ch sp, * rep from * to * twice more, 1 sc in each of 17 sc, ss in first of 3 ch. 19 sc on each side.

**Round 4:** Ss into 2-ch sp, 3 ch, 1 sc in same ch sp, * 1 sc in each of 19 sc, [1 sc, 2 ch, 1 sc] in 2-ch sp, * rep from * to * twice more, 1 sc in each of 19 sc, ss in first of 3 ch. 21 sc on each side.

**Round 5:** Ss into 2-ch sp, 3 ch, 1 sc in same ch sp, * 1 sc in each of 21 sc, [1 sc, 2 ch, 1 sc] in 2-ch sp, * rep from * to * twice more, 1 sc in each of 21 sc, ss in first of 3 ch. 23 sc on each side.

**Round 6:** Ss into 2-ch sp, 3 ch, 1 sc in same ch sp, * 1 sc in each of 23 sc, [1 sc, 2 ch, 1 sc] in 2-ch sp, * rep from * to * twice more, 1 sc in each of 23 sc, ss in first of 3 ch. 25 sc on each side.

Fasten off C.

## 26 PRIMROSE SQUARE
*directory view page 33*

A B C

**Skill level:** advanced
**Method of working:** in the round

**Key:**
- ◯ *Fingerwrap*
- ◠ *Chain*
- • *Slip stitch*
- + *Single*
- ⊤ *Double*
- ⊤ *Treble*
- ⊬ *2 singles together*
- ⋔ *Group as special abbreviation*
- ▷ *Join in new color*
- ◄ *Fasten off*

## METHOD

**Special abbreviations**
**1 gp (2 linked sts together):** yrh twice, insert as directed, [yrh, pull through 2 loops] twice, yrh, insert in lowest link of st just made, yrh, pull through link, yrh, pull through 2 loops, yrh, pull through rem 3 loops on hook; **5-ch P (5-ch picot):** 5 ch, ss in first of these 5 ch; **7-ch P (7-ch picot):** 7 ch, ss in first of these 7 ch.

**FIRST PRIMROSE**
Using A, make a fingerwrap.
**Round 1:** Ss into wrap, 1 ch, 4 sc into wrap, ss in first ch. 5 sts.
Fasten off A. Join B to any sc.
**Round 2:** 3 ch, 1 dc in first of these ch, 1 ch, 1 gp in same sc, * 3 ch, [1 gp, 1 ch, 1 gp] in next sc, * rep from * to * 3 more times, 3 ch, ss in first dc of round. Fasten off B. Join C to any 3-ch sp.
**Round 3:** 1 ch, 2 sc in same ch sp, * 2 sc tog over [same 3-ch sp and next 1-ch sp], 5-ch P, 2 sc tog over [same 1-ch sp and next 3-ch sp], 4 sc in same 3-ch sp, * rep from * to * once more, 2 sc tog as set, 7-ch P, 2 sc tog as set, 4 sc in same 3-ch sp, rep from * to * twice more, ending 1 sc in first ch sp, ss in first ch of round. Fasten off C.

**SECOND PRIMROSE**
Work as first primrose, joining to first primrose on last round by linking the second 5-ch P and the 7-ch P to corresponding picots (see page 21).

**THIRD PRIMROSE**
Work as first primrose, linking to second primrose as above.

**FOURTH PRIMROSE**
Work as first primrose without fastening off C, joining to first, second, and third primroses on last round by linking the second 5-ch P, the 7-ch P, and the next 5-ch P, forming a square. Do not fasten off. Rejoin C to last ss of round 3 of first primrose.

**Round 4:** Using C, 5 ch, * 1 dc in next sc, 3 ch, ss in 5-ch P, 3 ch, [1 tr, 3 ch, 1 tr] in st linking two 5-ch Ps, 3 ch, ss in next 5-ch P, 3 ch, 1 dc in 2nd of 4 sc, 2 ch, * rep from * to *, ending 3 ch, ss in 3rd of 5 ch.
**Round 5:** Ss into 2-ch sp, 5 ch, 2 dc in same ch sp, * 4 dc in each of next two 3-ch sps, 3 dc in 3-ch sp (between trs), 4 dc in each of next two 3-ch sps, [2 dc, 2 ch, 2 dc] in 2-ch sp at corner, * rep from * to * once more, ending 1 dc in first corner ch sp, ss in 3rd of 5 ch. 23 dc on each side.
**Round 6:** Ss into 2-ch sp, 3 ch, 1 sc in same ch sp, * 1 sc in each of 23 dc, [1 sc, 2 ch, 1 sc] in 2-ch sp at corner, * rep from * to * once more, ending 1 sc in first corner sp, ss in first of 3 ch. 25 sc on each side.
Fasten off C.

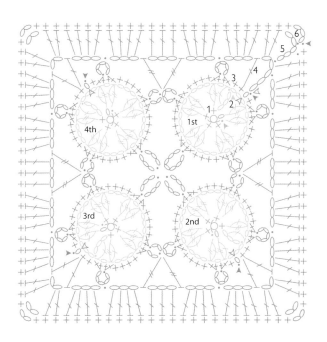

## 27 IRISH ROSE SQUARE
*directory view page 40*

A B

**Skill level:** advanced
**Method of working:** in the round

**Key:**
- ○ Chain
- • Slip stitch
- + Single
- ⊤ Half double
- ⊤ Double
- ⧘ Double treble
- ⊱ Back raised single
- ⊰ Back raised double
- ▷ Start/join in new color
- ◄ Fasten off

## METHOD

**Special abbreviations**
**PL (picot loop):** 4 ch, ss in 3$^{rd}$ ch from hook, 5 ch, ss in 3$^{rd}$ ch from hook, 1 ch.

**brdc (back-raised sc):** inserting hook from back, work sc around post of st on previous row.

**brdc (back-raised dc):** inserting hook from back, work dc around post of st on previous row.

Using A, make 6 ch, join into a ring with ss in first ch.
**Round 1:** 5 ch, [1 dc into ring, 2 ch] 7 times, ss in 3$^{rd}$ of 5 ch. 8 ch sps.
**Round 2:** Ss into 2-ch sp, [1 ch, 5 dc, 1 ch, 1 sc] in same ch sp, [1 sc, 1 ch, 5 dc, 1 ch, 1 sc] in each of seven 2-ch sps.
**Round 3:** Work behind round 2: 1 brsc in first dc of round 1, 5 ch, [1 brdc in next dc of round 1, 3 ch] 7 times, ss in 2$^{nd}$ of 5 ch.
**Round 4:** Ss into 3-ch sp, 2 ch, [7 dc, 1 ch, 1 sc] in same ch sp, [1 sc, 1 ch, 7 dc, 1 ch, 1 sc] in each of seven 3-ch sps, ss in first ch. Fasten off A. Join B from behind, around stem of any brsc of round 3.
**Round 5:** Work behind round 4: 7 ch, [1 brdc in next dc, 5 ch] 7 times, ss in 2$^{nd}$ of 7 ch.
**Round 6:** Ss in each of next 3 ch, 1 ch, [PL, 1 sc in next 5-ch sp] 7 times, PL, ss in first ch.

**Round 7:** 9 ch, 1 dtr in same place as base of these 9 ch, * [PL, 1 sc at center of next PL] twice, PL, [1 dtr, 4 ch, 1 dtr] in next sc (between 2 PL), * rep from * to * twice more, [PL, 1 sc in next sc] twice, PL, ss in 5$^{th}$ of 9 ch.
**Round 8:** Ss into 4-ch sp, 3 ch, [4 dc, 2 ch, 5 dc] in same ch sp, * 4 ch, 1 sc at center of next PL, [PL, 1 sc at center of next PL] twice, 4 ch, [5 dc, 2 ch, 5 dc] in 4-ch sp, * rep from * to * twice more, 4 ch, [PL, 1 sc at center of next PL] twice, 2 ch, 1 hdc in 3$^{rd}$ of 3 ch.
**Round 9:** Ss under hdc, 1 ch, * 5 ch, [1 sc, 2 ch, 1 sc] in 2-ch sp at corner, 5 ch, 1 sc in 4-ch sp, [2 ch, 1 sc in next picot] 4 times, 2 ch, 1 sc in 4-ch sp, * rep from * to * 3 more times omitting last sc of final repeat, ss in first ch.
**Round 10:** Ss under 5 ch, 1 ch, 4 sc in 5-ch sp, * [1 sc, 5 ch, ss in last sc made, 1 sc] in 2-ch sp at corner, 5 sc in 5-ch sp, 2 sc in next 2-ch sp, 3 sc in next 2-ch sp, [1 sc, 3 ch, ss in last sc made, 1 sc] in next 2-ch sp, 3 sc in next 2-ch sp, 2 sc in next 2-ch sp, 5 sc in 5-ch sp, * rep from * to * 3 more times omitting last 5 sc of final repeat, ss in first ch. Fasten off B.

Blocks may be joined using the joining with picots method, page 21.

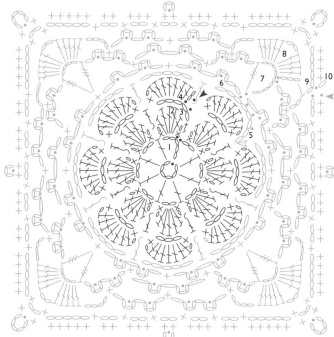

# 28 DAISY CHAIN SQUARE
*directory view page 32*

A  B

**Skill level:** intermediate
**Method of working:**
in the round

**Key:**
⌒ *Chain*
• *Slip stitch*
+ *Single*
† *Double*

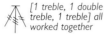 *[1 treble, 1 double treble, 1 treble] all worked together*

▷ *Start/join in new color*
◀ *Fasten off*

 *3 doubles together*

## METHOD

**Special abbreviation**
**3-ch P (3-ch picot):** 3 ch, ss in last sc.

Using A, make 5 ch, join into a ring with ss in first ch.
**Round 1:** 4 ch, [1 dc into ring, 1 ch] 7 times, ss in 3rd of 4 ch. 16 sts.
**Round 2:** 4 ch, [sk 1 ch, 3 dc in next dc, 1 ch] 7 times, sk 1 ch, 2 dc in first ch sp, ss in 3rd of 4 ch. 8 groups.
**Round 3:** Ss into 1-ch sp, 4 ch, [1 dc, 1 ch, 1 dc, 1 ch, 1 dc] in same ch sp, * sk 3 dc, [1 dc, 1 ch] 3 times in next ch sp, 1 dc in same ch sp, * rep from * to * 6 more times, ss in 3rd of 4 ch. 8 shell groups.
Fasten off A. Join B to 3rd ch sp of any shell group.
**Round 4:** 2 ch, 2 dc tog over [sp between next 2 dc, and first ch sp of next shell], * 3 ch, ss in next ch sp of same shell, 3 ch, 3 dc tog over [next ch sp of same shell, sp between next 2 dc, and first ch sp of next shell], * rep from * to * 6 more times, 3 ch, ss in next ch sp, 3 ch, ss in 2 dc tog at beg of round.
**Round 5:** 5 ch, [1 dc, 2 ch] 3 times in 2 dc tog, 1 dc in same place, * sk [3 ch, 1 ss, 3 ch], [1 dc, 2 ch] 4 times in 3 dc tog, 1 dc in same place, * rep from * to * 6 more times, ss in 3rd of 5 ch. 8 daisies.
Fasten off B. Join A to 4th ch sp of any daisy.

**Round 6:** 3 ch, [1 dtr between next 2 dc, tog with 1 tr in first 2-ch sp of next daisy], * 6 ch, 1 sc in next ch sp, 1 ch, 1 sc in next ch sp, 2 ch, 3 dc tog over [last ch sp of daisy, sp between 2 dc and first ch sp of next daisy], 2 ch, 1 sc in next ch sp, 1 ch, 1 sc in next ch sp, 6 ch, # [1 tr in last ch sp of daisy, tog with 1 dtr between next 2 dc, and 1 tr in first ch sp of next daisy], * rep from * to * twice more, then once again from * to #, ss in 2 sts tog at beg of round.
**Round 7:** 5 ch, 2 dc in 2 dc tog, * 3 ch, 1 sc in 6-ch sp, 3 ch, 1 dc in 1-ch sp, 3 ch, 1 sc in 3 dc tog, 3 ch, 1 dc in 1-ch sp, 3 ch, 1 sc in 6-ch sp, 3 ch, # [2 dc, 2 ch, 2 dc] in 3 sts tog at corner, * rep from * to * twice more, then once again from * to #, 1 dc in same place as beg of round, ss in 3rd of 5 ch.
**Round 8:** Ss into 2-ch sp, 6 ch, 1 sc in same ch sp, * 1 sc in each of 2 dc, 3 sc in 3-ch sp, 3-ch P, [3 sc in next 3-ch sp] twice, 3-ch P, [3 sc in next 3-ch sp] twice, 3-ch P, 3 sc in next 3-ch sp, 1 sc in each of 2 dc #, [1 sc, 5 ch, 1 sc] in 2-ch sp at corner, * rep from * to * twice more, then once again from * to #, ss in first of 6 ch.
Fasten off A.

Blocks may be joined using the joining with picots method, page 21.

## 29 POPPY SQUARE
directory view page 50

A  B  C

**Skill level:** intermediate
**Method of working:**
in the round

**Key:**

◯ *Chain*

• *Slip stitch*

+ *Single*

⌶ *Half double in front loop*

┃ *Double*

⊤ *Double in back loop*

⊤ *Treble*

⊧ *Double treble*

▷ *Start/join in new color*

◀ *Fasten off*

## METHOD

Using A, make 4 ch, join with ss in first ch.

**Round 1:** 1 ch, 7 sc into ring, ss in first ch. 8 sts.

**Round 2:** 4 ch, [1 hdc in front loop of next sc, 1 ch] 7 times, ss in 3rd of 4 ch.
Fasten off A. Join B to back loop of any hdc.

**Round 3:** 3 ch, [2 dc in 1-ch sp, 1 dc in back loop of next hdc] 7 times, 2 dc in 1-ch sp, ss in 3rd of 3 ch.

**Round 4:** [3 ch, 1 tr in next hdc, 2 dtr in next hdc, 1 dtr in next hdc, 2 dtr in next hdc, 1 tr in next hdc, 3 ch, ss in next hdc] 4 times, working final ss in same place as base of first 3 ch. 4 petals.
Fasten off B. Join C to center tr of any petal.

**Round 5:** 5 ch, 1 dc in same tr, * 5 ch, [1 dc, 3 ch, 1 dc] in ss between petals, 5 ch, # [1 dc, 2 ch, 1 dc] in center tr of next petal, * rep from * to * twice more, then once again from * to #, ss in 3rd of 5 ch.

**Round 6:** Ss into 2-ch sp, 5 ch, 1 dc in same ch sp, * 5 ch, 1 sc in 5-ch sp, [3 dc, 1 ch, 3 dc] in next 3-ch sp, 1 sc in next 5-ch sp, 5 ch, #

[1 dc, 2 ch, 1 dc] in next 2-ch sp, * rep from * to * twice more, then once again from * to #, ss in 3rd of 5 ch.

**Round 7:** Ss into 2-ch sp, 5 ch, 1 dc in same ch sp, * 5 ch, 1 sc in next 5-ch sp, 5 ch, 1 sc in next 1-ch sp, 5 ch, 1 sc in next 5-ch sp, 5 ch, # [1 dc, 2 ch, 1 dc] in next 2-ch sp, * rep from * to * twice more, then once again from * to #, ss in 3rd of 5 ch.

**Round 8:** Ss into 2-ch sp, 5 ch, 1 dc in same ch sp, * [5 ch, 1 sc in next 5-ch sp] 4 times, 5 ch, # [1 dc, 2 ch, 1 dc] in next 2-ch sp, * rep from * to * twice more, then once again from * to #, ss in 3rd of 5 ch.

**Round 9:** Ss into 2-ch sp, 5 ch, 1 dc in same ch sp, * 4 dc in next 5-ch sp, [5 dc in next 5-ch sp] 3 times, 4 dc in next 5-ch sp, # [1 dc, 2 ch, 1 dc] in next 2-ch sp, * rep from * to * twice more, then once again from * to #, ss in 3rd of 5 ch.
25 dc on each side.
Fasten off C.

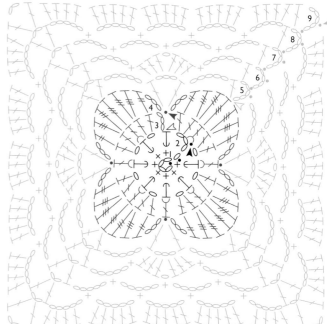

## 30 SNEEZEWORT SQUARE
directory view page 50

**Skill level:** intermediate
**Method of working:**
in the round

**Key:**

⌒ *Chain*

• *Slip stitch*

+ *Single*

⊤ *Half double*

⸶ *Double*

▷ *Start/join in new color*

◄ *Fasten off*

## METHOD

Using A, make 12 ch, join into a ring with ss in first ch.

**Round 1:** 1 ch, 23 sc into ring, ss in first ch. 24 sts.

**Round 2:** 1 ch, * 1 sc in next sc, 3 ch, ss in last sc made, # 1 sc in next sc, * rep from * to * 10 more times, then once again from * to #, ss in first ch. 12 picots.
Fasten off A. Join B to any sc between 2 picots.

**Round 3:** 6 ch, [sk 1 picot, 1 sc in next sc, 5 ch] 11 times, sk 1 picot, ss in first of 6 ch. 12 loops.

**Round 4:** 3 ch, * [1 hdc, 1 sc, 1 ch, 1 sc, 1 hdc] in 5-ch loop, # 1 dc in next sc, * rep from * to * 10 more times, then once again from * to #, ss in 3$^{rd}$ of 3 ch. 12 petals.
Fasten off B. Join C to 1-ch sp at center of any petal.

**Round 5:** 6 ch, [1 sc in next 1-ch sp, 5 ch] 11 times, ss in first of 6 ch. 12 ch sps.

**Round 6:** 5 ch, 3 dc in same place as base of these 5 ch, * [1 sc in next 5-ch sp, 5 ch] twice, 1 sc in next 5-ch sp, # [3 dc, 2 ch, 3 dc] in next sc, * rep from * to * twice more, then once again from * to #, 2 dc in same place as base of first 5 ch, ss in 3$^{rd}$ of these 5 ch.

**Round 7:** Ss into 2-ch sp, 5 ch, 3 dc in same ch sp, * [5 ch, 1 sc in next 5-ch sp] twice, 5 ch, # [3 dc, 2 ch, 3 dc] in next 2-ch sp, * rep from * to * twice more, then once again from * to #, 2 dc in first 2-ch sp, ss in 3$^{rd}$ of 5 ch.

**Round 8:** Ss into 2-ch sp, 5 ch, 3 dc in same ch sp, * 5 ch, 1 sc in next 5-ch sp, [3 dc, 1 ch, 3 dc] in next 5-ch sp, 1 sc in next 5-ch sp, 5 ch, # [3 dc, 2 ch, 3 dc] in next 2-ch sp, * rep from * to * twice more, then once again from * to #, 2 dc in first 2-ch sp, ss in 3$^{rd}$ of 5 ch.
Fasten off C.

## 31 SPANISH POPPY SQUARE
*directory view page 42*

A B

**Skill level:** intermediate
**Method of working:** in the round

**Key:**
◠ Chain
• Slip stitch
+ Single
⊤ Half double
† Double
╪ Double treble
▷ Start/join in new color
◀ Fasten off

## METHOD

Using A, make 6 ch, join into a ring with ss in first ch.

**Round 1:** 1 ch, 15 sc into ring, ss in first ch. 16 sts.

**Round 2:** 1 ch, 1 sc in next sc, * [1 sc, 11 ch, 1 sc] in next sc, 1 sc in each of 3 sc, * rep from * to * twice more, [1 sc, 11 ch, 1 sc] in next sc, 1 sc in next sc, ss in first ch. 4 petals.

**Round 3:** 1 ch, * sk 2 sc, [2 hdc, 17 dc, 2 hdc] into 11-ch loop, sk 2 sc, 1 sc in next sc, * rep from * to * 3 more times omitting last sc of final repeat, ss in first ch. Fasten off A. Join B to sc between any 2 petals.

**Round 4:** 10 ch, ss in 6th ch from hook, * 3 ch, sk 5 sts, 1 sc in next dc, [5 ch, sk 4 dc, 1 sc in next dc] twice, 3 ch, sk 5 sts, 1 dtr in next sc (between petals), 5 ch, ss in top of dtr just made, * rep from * to * twice more, 3 ch, sk 5 sts, 1 sc in next dc, [5 ch, sk 4 dc, 1 sc in next dc] twice, 1 ch, 1 hdc in 5th of 10 ch.

**Round 5:** 1 ch, * [2 hdc, 9 dc, 2 hdc] in 5-ch loop, 1 sc in next 3-ch sp, [5 ch, 1 sc in next 3-ch sp] 3 times, * rep from * to * omitting last sc of final repeat, ss in first ch.

**Round 6:** 3 ch, * 3 ch, sk 3 sts, 1 sc in next dc, 3 ch, sk 2 dc, [1 sc, 3 ch, 1 sc] in next dc, 3 ch, sk 2 dc, 1 sc in next dc, 3 ch, sk 3 sts, 1 dc in next sc, [3 ch, 1 sc in next ch sp] 3 times, 3 ch, 1 dc in next sc, * rep from * to * 3 more times omitting last dc of final repeat, ss in 3rd of 3 ch.

**Round 7:** Ss in each of 2 ch, 4 ch, 1 sc in next ch sp, * 3 ch, [1 sc, 3 ch, 1 sc] in 3-ch loop at corner, [3 ch, 1 sc in next ch sp] 8 times, * rep from * to * twice more, 3 ch, [1 sc, 3 ch, 1 sc] in corner loop, [3 ch, 1 sc in next ch sp] 6 times, 3 ch, ss in first of 4 ch. Fasten off B.

# 32 RUFFLED FLOWER SQUARE
*directory view page 47*

A  B

**Skill level:** advanced
**Method of working:** in the round

**Key:**
- ⌒ Chain
- • Slip stitch
- + Single
- ‡ Treble

 4 trebles around stem

▷ Start/join in new color
◄ Fasten off

## METHOD

Using A, make 10 ch, join into a ring with ss in first ch.

**Round 1:** 7 ch, [1 tr into ring, 3 ch] 11 times, ss in 4th of 7 ch. 12 ch sps.

**Round 2:** Ss into 3-ch sp, 4 ch, 3 tr in same ch sp, * 4 tr around stem of next tr (working down the stem toward the center), 1 tr in center ring, 4 tr around stem of next tr (working up the stem away from the center), (3-ch sp has been skipped), # 4 tr in next 3-ch sp, * rep from * to * 4 more times, then once again from * to #, ss in 4th of 4 ch.

Fasten off A. Join B to any empty 3-ch sp behind round 2.

**Round 3:** 1 ch, 2 sc in same ch sp, [3 ch, 3 sc in next empty 3-ch sp] 5 times, 3 ch, ss in first ch of round.

**Round 4:** 1 ch, 2 sc in next sc, 1 sc in next sc, * 4 sc in 3-ch sp, 1 sc in next sc, 2 sc in next sc, 1 sc in next sc, * rep from * to * 4 more times, 4 sc in 3-ch sp, ss in first ch.

**Round 5:** 4 ch, [sk 2 sc, 1 sc in next sc, 3 ch] 15 times, ss in first of 4 ch. 16 ch sps.

**Round 6:** Ss into rem 3-ch sp, 5 ch, [1 sc in next 3-ch sp, 4 ch] 15 times, ss in first of 5 ch.

**Round 7:** Ss into next ch, ss into rem 3-ch sp, 6 ch, [1 sc in next 4-ch sp, 5 ch] 15 times, ss in first of 6 ch.

**Round 8:** Ss into each of 2 ch, ss into rem 3-ch sp, 6 ch, 3 tr in same ch sp, * 2 ch, 1 sc in next 5-ch sp, [5 ch, 1 sc in next 5-ch sp] twice, 2 ch, # [3 tr; 2 ch, 3 tr] in next 5-ch sp, * rep from * to * twice more, then once again from * to #, 2 tr in first ch sp, ss in 4th of 6 ch.

**Round 9:** Ss into 2-ch sp, 6 ch, 3 tr in same ch sp, * 1 tr in each of 3 tr; 2 tr in 2-ch sp, 2 ch, 1 sc in next 5-ch sp, 5 ch, 1 sc in next 5-ch sp, 2 ch, 2 tr in 2-ch sp, 1 tr in each of 3 tr; # [3 tr; 2 ch, 3 tr] in 2-ch sp, * rep from * to * twice more, then once again from * to #, 2 tr in first ch sp, ss in 4th of 6 ch.

Fasten off B.

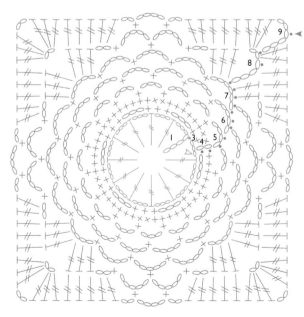

## 33 STONECROP SQUARE
*directory view page 49*

**Skill level:** intermediate
**Method of working:** in decreasing rows

**Key:**
⌒ Chain
⋋⋌ 2 singles together
† Treble
Petal 4: 2 trebles together in same place
Petal 5: 3 trebles together in same place
Petals 1, 2, and 3: 8 trebles together as given
▷ Start
◀ Fasten off

## METHOD

Make 54 ch.

**Row 1:** 1 tr in 5th ch from hook, 1 tr in each of 17 ch, 3 ch, 8 tr tog as follows: [2 tr in top of last tr worked, sk 3 ch, 3 tr in next ch, sk 5 ch, 3 tr in next ch] (petals 1, 2, and 3 made), 4 ch, 2 tr tog in first of these 4 ch, (petal 4 made), sk next 3 base ch, 1 tr in each of 19 ch to end.

**Row 2:** 4 ch, sk first tr, 1 tr in each of 18 tr, sk 4th petal, 3 tr tog in ch closing 8 tr, sk first petal, 1 tr in each of 18 tr, 1 tr in 4th of 4 ch. 39 sts.

**Row 3:** 4 ch, sk first tr, 1 tr in each of 12 tr, * 3 ch, 8 tr tog as follows: [2 tr in top of last tr worked, sk 3 tr, 3 tr in next ch, sk 5 sts, 3 tr in next ch] (petals 1, 2, and 3 made), 4 ch, 2 tr tog in first of these 4 ch (petal 4 made), sk 3 tr, * 1 tr in each of 12 tr, 1 tr in 4th of 4 ch.

**Row 4:** 4 ch, sk first tr, 1 tr in each of 12 tr, * sk 4th petal, 3 tr tog in ch closing 8 tr, sk first petal (petal 5 made), * 1 tr in each of 12 tr, 1 tr in 4th of 4 ch. 27 sts.

**Row 5:** 4 ch, sk first tr, 1 tr in each of 6 tr, work as row 3 from * to *, 1 tr in each of 6 tr, 1 tr in 4th of 4 ch.

**Row 6:** 4 ch, sk first tr, 1 tr in each of 6 tr, work as row 4 from * to *, 1 tr in each of 6 tr, 1 tr in 4th of 4 ch. 15 sts.

**Row 7:** 4 ch, work as row 3 from * to *, 1 tr in 4th of 4 ch.

**Row 8:** 4 ch, 3 tr tog in ch closing 8 tr tog, 1 tr in 4th of 4 ch. 3 sts.

**Row 9:** 1 ch, 2 sc tog over [top of 3 tr tog and 4th of 4 ch]. Fasten off.

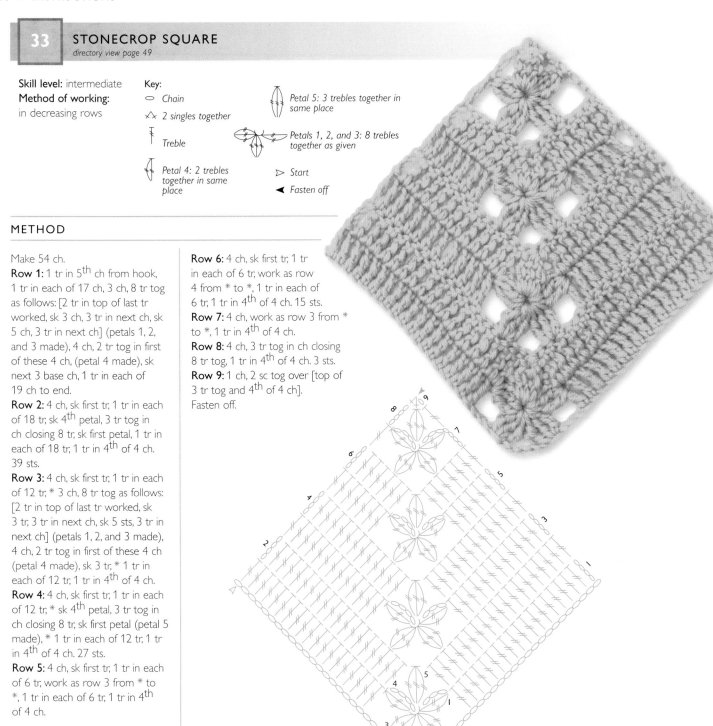

## 34 SUNFLOWER SQUARE
*directory view page 51*

A B C

**Skill level:** easy
**Method of working:** in the round

**Key:**
⌒ Chain
• Slip stitch
+ Single
⋋⋌ 2 singles together
† Double

 5 double trebles together in back loop
▷ Start/join in new color
◀ Fasten off

## METHOD

**Special abbreviation**
**3-ch P (3-ch picot):** 3 ch, ss in st at base of these 3 ch.

Using A, make 5 ch, join into a ring with ss in first ch.
**Round 1:** 3 ch, 15 dc into ring, ss into 3rd of 3 ch.
Fasten off A. Join B to space between any 2 dc.
**Round 2:** 1 ch, [2 sc in space between next 2 dc] 15 times, 1 sc in first sp, ss in first ch.
Fasten off B. Join C to back loop of any sc.
**Round 3:** 5 ch, 4 dtr tog in back loops of next 4 sc, * 6 ch, 5 dtr tog over back loops of [same sc as last insertion and foll 4 sc], 7 ch, 5 dtr tog as before, * rep from * to * 2 more times, 6 ch, 5 dtr tog making last insertion in same place as base of 5 ch, 7 ch, ss in top of 4 dtr tog. 8 petals made.
Fasten off C. Join B to any 7-ch sp.

**Round 4:** 4 ch, ss in first of these 4 ch, * 4 sc in same 7-ch sp, 1 sc in top of petal, 7 sc in 6-ch sp, 1 sc in next petal, 5 sc in 7-ch sp, 3-ch P, * rep from * to * ending 4 sc in first 7-ch sp, ss in first of 4 ch.
**Round 5:** Ss into 3-ch P, 5 ch, 1 dc in same P, * 1 dc in each of 17 sc, [1 dc, 2 ch, 1 dc] in 3-ch P, * rep from * to * twice more, 1 dc in each of 17 sc, ss in 3rd of 5 ch. 19 dc on each side.
**Round 6:** Ss into 2-ch sp, 5 ch, 1 dc in same 2-ch sp, * 1 ch, [1 dc in next dc, 1 ch, sk 1 dc] 9 times, 1 dc in next dc, 1 ch, # [1 dc, 2 ch, 1 dc] in 2-ch sp, * rep from * to * twice more, then once again from * to #, ss in 3rd of 5 ch.
**Round 7:** Ss into 2-ch sp, 3 ch, 1 dc in same 2-ch sp, 1 sc in each dc and 1-ch sp, and [1 sc, 2 ch, 1 sc] in 2-ch sp at each corner, ending ss in first of 3 ch. 25 sc on each side.
Fasten off B.

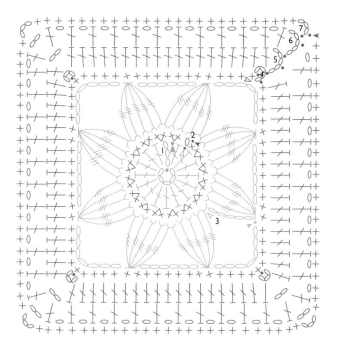

## 35 BOBBLE SQUARE
*directory view page 37*

**Skill level:** easy
**Method of working:** in rows

**Key:**

⬭ *Chain*

+ *Single*

 *Bobble of 4 doubles together*

▷ *Start*

◀ *Fasten off*

## METHOD

**Special abbreviation**
**B (make bobble):** 4 dc tog in same place.

Make 28 ch.
**Row 1:** 1 sc in 3$^{rd}$ ch from hook, 1 sc in each of 23 ch. 27 sts.
**Row 2:** 1 ch, sk first sc, 1 sc in each st, ending 1 sc in first ch. 27 sts.
**Rows 3–5:** As row 2.
**Row 6:** 1 ch, sk first sc, 1 sc in each of 10 sc, [B in next sc, 1 sc in next sc] twice, B in next sc, 11 sc as set to end.
**Row 7:** As row 2.
**Row 8:** 1 ch, sk first sc, 1 sc in each of 7 sc, B in next sc, 9 sc as set, B in next sc, 8 sc as set to end.
**Row 9:** As row 2.
**Row 10:** 1 ch, sk first sc, 1 sc in each of 5 sc, B in next sc, 13 sc as set, B in next sc, 6 sc as set to end.
**Row 11:** As row 2.

**Row 12:** 1 ch, sk first sc, 1 sc in each of 4 sc, B in next sc, 15 sc as set, B in next sc, 5 sc as set to end.
**Row 13:** As row 2.
**Row 14:** 1 ch, sk first sc, 1 sc in each of 4 sc, [B in next sc, 7 sc as set] twice, B in next sc, 5 sc as set to end.
**Row 15:** As row 2.
**Row 16:** As row 12.
**Row 17:** As row 2.
**Row 18:** As row 10.
**Row 19:** As row 2.
**Row 20:** As row 8.
**Row 21:** As row 2.
**Row 22:** As row 6.
**Rows 23–27:** As row 2.
Fasten off.

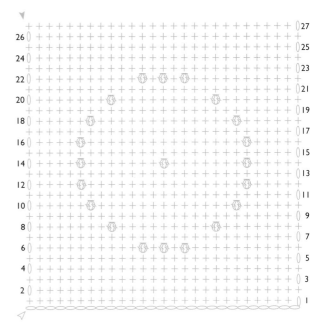

**36** TULIP SQUARE
*directory view page 35*

A B C

**Skill level:** intermediate
**Method of working:** in rows

**Key:**
- ⌒ *Chain*
- • *Slip stitch*
- + *Single*
- ▷ *Start/join in new color*
- ◀ *Fasten off*

## METHOD

**Special abbreviation**
**chg to A (or B or C):** changing to A (or B or C) for the final "yrh, pull through" of the last st worked.

Using A, make 26 ch.
**Row 1:** 1 sc in 2nd ch from hook, 1 sc in each of 24 ch. 25 sc. (Turning ch does not count as a st in this pattern.)
**Row 2:** 1 ch, 1 sc in first sc, 1 sc in each sc to end. 25 sc.
On rows 3–23, enclose color not in use by working over it until it is required.
**Row 3:** Read chart row 3 from right to left: In A, 1 ch, 1 sc in each of 11 sc, chg to B, 1 sc in each of 3 sc, chg to A, 1 sc in each of 11 sc.

**Row 4:** Read chart row 4 from left to right: In A, 1 ch, 1 sc in each of 9 sc, chg to B, 1 sc in each of 7 sc, chg to A, 1 sc in each of 9 sc.
Continue reading from chart rows 5–23 in this way, changing colors as indicated.
**Rows 24–25:** In A, as row 2.
Fasten off A. Join B to last sc of row 25.
**Edging round:** 1 ch, 1 sc in each of 24 sc, 2 ch, 1 sc in side edge of each of 25 rows, 2 ch, 1 sc in base of each of 25 sts, 2 ch, 1 sc in side edge of each of 25 rows, 2 ch, ss in first ch. 25 sc on each side.
Fasten off B.

### MIX AND MATCH: 36 + 26

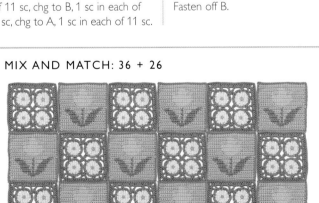

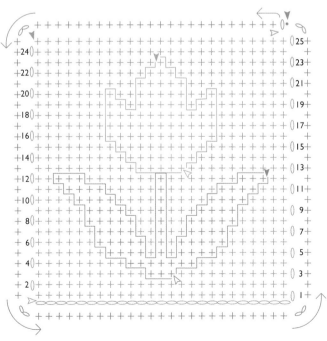

## 37 OFF-CENTER SQUARE
*directory view page 47*

**Skill level:** intermediate
**Method of working:**
in the round and in rows

**Key:**

⌒ *Chain*

• *Slip stitch*

+ *Single*

⊤ *Half double*

⊤ *Double*

⊤ *Treble*

⫙ *4 trebles together*

⊤ *Double treble*

⫙ *4 double trebles together*

▷ *Start/rejoin*

◄ *Fasten off*

↵ *Direction of working*

## METHOD

Make 8 ch, join into a ring with ss in first ch.

**Round 1:** 1 ch, [3 sc, 4 hdc, 4 dc, 4 hdc] into ring, ss in first ch. 16 sts.

**Round 2:** 3 ch, 3 tr tog inserting hook [once in same place as base of these 3 ch, twice in next sc], (from now on, insert hook twice in each st of round 1), 4 ch, 4 tr tog over next 2 sc, 5 ch, 4 dtr tog over next 2 hdc, 6 ch, 4 dtr tog over next 2 hdc, [7 ch, 4 dtr tog over next 2 dc] twice, 7 ch, 4 dtr tog over next 2 hdc, 6 ch, 4 dtr tog over next 2 hdc, 5 ch, ss in ch closing 3 tr tog. 8 petals made: 2 small, 2 medium, 2 large, 2 medium.

**Round 3:** Work all sc into ch closing a petal: 12 ch, 1 sc in 2$^{nd}$ petal, 5 ch, 1 sc in 3$^{rd}$ petal, 10 ch, 1 sc in 4th petal, 7 ch, 1 sc in 5$^{th}$ petal, 10 ch, 1 sc in 6$^{th}$ petal, 7 ch, 1 sc in 7$^{th}$ petal, 10 ch, 1 sc in 8$^{th}$ petal, 5 ch, ss in first of 12 ch.

**Round 4:** Ss in each of 6 ch, 3 ch, 5 sc in same ch sp, 1 ch, sk 1 sc, 5 sc in 5-ch sp, 1 ch, sk 1 sc, [6 sc, 2 ch, 4 sc] in 10-ch sp, 1 ch, sk 1 sc, 7 sc in 7-ch sp, 1 ch, sk 1 sc, [5 sc, 2 ch, 5 sc] in 10-ch sp, 1 ch, sk 1 sc, 7 sc in 7-ch sp, 1 ch, sk 1 sc, [4 sc, 2 ch, 6 sc] in 10-ch sp, 1 ch, sk 1 sc, 5 sc in 5-ch sp, 1 ch, 4 sc in first ch sp, ss in first of 3 ch. 18 sts on each side of square.

Fasten off and rejoin to 2-ch sp at next corner.

Now work in rows on two sides only:

**Row 1:** 1 ch, 1 sc in each sc and 1-ch sp to next corner, [1 sc, 2 ch, 1 sc] in 2-ch sp, 1 sc in each sc and 1-ch sp to next corner, 1 sc in 2-ch sp, turn. 20 sts on each of 2 sides.

**Row 2:** 1 ch, sk first sc, 1 sc in each sc to next corner, [1 sc, 2 ch, 1 sc] in 2-ch sp, 1 sc in each sc ending 1 sc in 1 ch, turn. 21 sc on each side.

**Row 3:** As row 2. 22 sc on each side.

**Row 4:** As row 2. 23 sc on each side.

Now work all around:

**Final round:** 3 ch, 1 sc in each of 23 sc to corner, [1 sc, 2 ch, 1 sc] in 2-ch sp, 1 sc in each of 22 sc, [2 sc, 2 ch, 1 sc] in 1 ch, 4 sc in side edge of 4 rows, 1 sc in 2-ch sp, 1 sc in each sc and 1-ch sp (making 18 sc), [1 sc, 2 ch, 1 sc] in 2-ch sp, 1 sc in each sc and 1-ch sp (making 18 sc), 1 sc in 2-ch sp, 4 sc in side edge of 4 rows, ss in first of 3 ch. 25 sc on each of 4 sides. Fasten off.

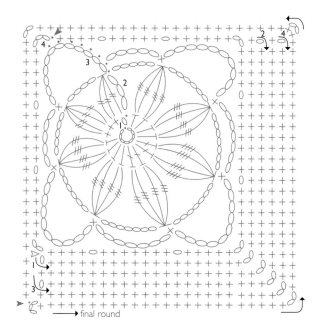

final round

## 38 ROSEBUD SQUARE
*directory view page 44*

**Skill level:** easy
**Method of working:** in decreasing rows

**Key:**
⌒ *Chain*
+ *Single*
T *Double*
⋏ *2 doubles together*
○ *Bobble of 4 doubles together*

🙡 *2 trebles together*
▷ *Start*
◀ *Fasten off*

## METHOD

**Special abbreviations**
**LG (leaf group):** [2 tr tog, 1 ch, 1 dc, 1 ch, 2 tr tog] all worked into 1 st, as given.
**B (bobble):** 4 dc tog in same place.

Make 57 ch.
**Row 1 (WS):** 1 sc in 3rd ch from hook, 1 sc in each of 25 ch, sk 2 ch, 1 sc in each of 27 ch to end. 54 sts.
**Row 2:** 3 ch, * sk 3 sc, [LG in next sc, 1 ch, sk 5 sc] 3 times, LG in next sc, * sk 3 sc, 1 dc in next sc, sk 2 sc, 1 dc in next sc, rep from * to * once more, sk 2 sc, 1 dc in next ch. 8 patterns.
**Row 3:** 1 ch, sk first dc, * [1 sc in 2 tr tog, 1 sc in 1-ch sp, B in next dc, 1 sc in 1-ch sp, 1 sc in 2 tr tog, 1 sc in 1-ch sp] 3 times, 1 sc in 2 tr tog, 1 sc in 1-ch sp, B in next dc, 1 sc in 1-ch sp, 1 sc in 2 tr tog, * sk 2 dc, rep from * to * once more, 1 sc in 3rd of 3 ch. 48 sts.
**Row 4:** 4 ch, 2 tr tog in first sc, [1 ch, sk 5 sts, LG in next sc] 3 times, sk [2 sc, B], 1 dc in next sc, sk 2 sc, 1 dc in next sc, sk [B, 2 sc], [LG in next sc, 1 ch, sk 5 sts] 3 times, [2 tr tog, 1 ch, 1 dc] in 1 ch. 6 patterns plus two half-patterns.
**Row 5:** 1 ch, sk first dc, 1 sc in 1-ch sp, 1 sc in 2 tr tog, * [1 sc in 1-ch sp, 1 sc in 2 tr tog, 1 sc in 1-ch sp, B in dc, 1 sc in 1-ch sp, 1 sc in 2 tr tog] 3 times, * sk 2 dc, rep from * to * once more, 1 sc in 1-ch sp, 1 sc in 2 tr tog, 1 sc in 1-ch sp, 1 sc in 3rd of 4 ch. 42 sts.

**Row 6:** 3 ch, sk 3 sc, * [LG in next sc, 1 ch, sk 5 sts] twice, LG in next sc, * sk [2 sc, B], 1 dc in next sc, sk 2 sc, 1 dc in next sc, sk [B, 2 sc], rep from * to * once more, sk 2 sc, 1 dc in next ch. 6 patterns.
**Row 7:** 1 ch, sk first dc, * [1 sc in 2 tr tog, 1 sc in 1-ch sp, B in next dc, 1 sc in 1-ch sp, 1 sc in 2 tr tog, 1 sc in 1-ch sp] twice, 1 sc in 2 tr tog, 1 sc in 1-ch sp, B in next dc, 1 sc in 1-ch sp, 1 sc in 2 tr tog, * sk 2 dc, rep from * to * once more, 1 sc in 3rd of 3 ch. 36 sts.
**Row 8:** 3 ch, sk first sc, 1 dc in each of 2 sc, [1 dc in B, 1 dc in each of 5 sc] twice, 2 dc tog over [B and foll sc], sk 2 dc, 2 dc tog over [next sc and foll B], [1 dc in each of 5 sc, 1 dc in B] twice, 1 dc in each of 2 sc, 1 dc in 1 ch. 32 sts.
**Row 9:** 1 ch, sk first sc, 1 sc in each dc to 2 dc tog, [sk 2 dc tog] twice, 1 sc in each dc ending 1 sc in 3rd of 3 ch. 30 sts.
**Row 10:** 3 ch, sk first sc, 1 dc in each sc to 3 sc before corner, 2 dc tog over next 2 sc, sk 2 sc, 2 dc tog over next 2 sc, 1 dc in each sc ending 1 dc in 1 ch. 26 sts.
**Rows 11–16:** Rep rows 9–10 three more times. 8 sts.
**Row 17:** As row 9. 6 sts.
**Row 18:** 2 ch, sk first sc, 3 dc tog over [next and foll 3rd sc, and 1 ch].
Fasten off.

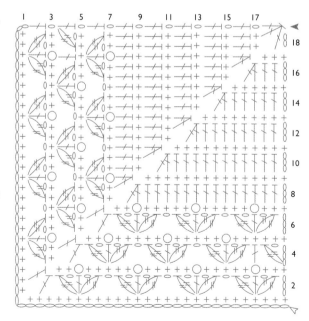

## 39 FILET FLOWER SQUARE
*directory view page 35*

**Skill level:** easy
**Method of working:**
in the round

**Key:**

⌒ *Chain*

• *Slip stitch*

+ *Single*

† *Double*

⅄ *2 doubles together*

◄ *Fasten off*

## METHOD

Make 6 ch, join into a ring with ss in first ch.

**Round 1:** 1 ch, 11 sc into ring, ss in first ch. 12 sts.

**Round 2:** 3 ch, 4 dc in same place as base of 4 ch, [3 ch, sk 2 sc, 5 dc in next sc] 3 times, 3 ch, ss in 3rd of 3 ch at beg of round.

**Round 3:** 3 ch, 1 dc in next dc, 5 dc in next dc, 1 dc in each of 2 dc, * 3 ch, sk 3 ch, 1 dc in each of 2 dc, 5 dc in next dc, 1 dc in each of 2 dc, * rep from * to * twice more, 3 ch, sk 3 ch, ss in 3rd of 3 ch. 9 dc at each corner.

**Round 4:** 3 ch, 1 dc in each of 3 dc, 5 dc in next dc, 1 dc in each of 4 dc, * 3 ch, sk 3 ch, 1 dc in each of 4 dc, 5 dc in next dc, 1 dc in each of 4 dc, * rep from * to * twice more, 3 ch, sk 3 ch, ss in 3rd of 3 ch. 13 dc at each corner.

**Round 5:** 2 ch, 1 dc in each of 4 dc, * 2 dc tog over next 2 dc, 7 ch, 2 dc tog over [same dc as last insertion, and next dc], 1 dc in each of 3 dc, 2 dc tog over next 2 dc, 5 ch, sk 3 ch, # 2 dc tog over next 2 dc, 1 dc in each of 3 dc, * rep from * to * twice more, then once again from * to #, ss in first dc (omitting first 2 ch).

**Round 6:** 2 ch, 1 dc in each of 2 dc, * 2 dc tog over next 2 sts, 3 ch, sk 2 ch, 1 dc in next ch, 3 ch, sk 1 ch, 1 dc in next ch, 3 ch, sk 2 ch, 2 dc tog over next 2 sts, 1 dc in next dc, 2 dc tog over next 2 sts, 3 ch, sk 2 ch, 1 dc in next ch, 3 ch, sk 2 ch, # 2 dc tog over next 2 sts, 1 dc in next dc, * rep from * to * twice more, then once again from * to #, ss in first dc.

**Round 7:** 4 ch, sk first 2 dc, 1 dc in 2 dc tog, 1 ch, sk 1 ch, 1 dc in next ch, 1 ch, sk 1 ch, 1 dc in next dc, * 5 ch, sk 3 ch, 1 dc in next dc, [1 ch, sk 1 st, 1 dc in next st] 10 times, * rep from * to * twice more, 5 ch, sk 3 ch, 1 dc in next dc, [1 ch, sk 1 st, 1 dc in next st] 6 times, 1 ch, sk 1 st, ss in 3rd of 4 ch. Ten 1-ch sps on each side.

**Round 8:** 1 ch, * 1 sc in each 1-ch sp and in each dc to corner; [2 sc, 3 ch, 2 sc] in 5-ch sp, * rep from * to * 3 more times, 1 sc in each 1-ch sp and in each dc, ending ss in first ch. 25 sc on each side.
Fasten off.

# 40 DANDELION DIAMOND
*directory view page 36*

A B

**Skill level:** easy
**Method of working:**
in rows and in the round

**Key:**
⌒ *Chain*
• *Slip stitch*
+ *Single*
⊤ *Double*
⊤ *Treble*
⅄ *4 trebles together*
▷ *Start/join in new color*
◀ *Fasten off*

## METHOD

Using A, make 27 ch.
**Row 1:** 4 tr tog over [6th, 8th, 11th, and 13th] ch from hook, 4 ch, sk 1 ch, 1 sc in next ch, turn.
**Row 2:** [1 ch, 1 tr] 4 times in ch closing 4 tr tog, 1 ch, sk [4 tr tog, 3 ch], 1 sc in next ch. 1 flower made.
**Row 3:** 9 ch, 4 tr tog over [6th and 8th ch from hook, last 1-ch sp of row 2, and foll 1-ch sp], 4 ch, 1 sc in next 1-ch sp, 3 ch, 4 tr tog over [next two 1-ch sps, 2nd and 4th unworked base ch], 4 ch, sk 1 base ch, 1 sc in next ch.
**Row 4:** * [1 ch, 1 tr] 4 times in ch closing 4 tr tog, 1 ch, sk [4 tr tog, 3 ch], * ss in next sc, rep from * to * once more, 1 sc in next ch.
2 flowers made.
**Row 5:** 9 ch, 4 tr tog over [6th and 8th ch from hook, last 1-ch sp of row 2, and foll 1-ch sp], 4 ch, 1 sc in next 1-ch sp, 3 ch, 4 tr tog over next four 1-ch sps, 4 ch, 1 sc in next 1-ch sp, 3 ch, 4 tr tog over [next two 1-ch sps, 2nd and 4th unworked base ch], 4 ch, sk 1 base ch, 1 sc in next ch.
**Row 6:** * [1 ch, 1 tr] 4 times in ch closing 4 tr tog, 1 ch, sk [4 tr tog, 3 ch], # ss in next sc, * rep from * to * once more, then once again from * to #, 1 sc in next ch.
3 flowers made.

**Row 7:** Ss in each of next 4 sts, 1 dc in next 1-ch sp, * 3 ch, 4 tr tog over next four 1-ch sps, 4 ch, 1 sc in next 1-ch sp, * rep from * to * once more, turn.
**Row 8:** * [1 ch, 1 tr] 4 times in ch closing 4 tr tog, 1 ch, sk [4 tr tog, 3 ch], ss in next sc, * rep from * to * once more. 2 flowers made.
**Row 9:** Ss in each of next 4 sts, 1 sc in next 1-ch sp, 3 ch, 4 tr tog over next four 1-ch sps, 4 ch, 1 sc in next 1-ch sp, turn.
**Row 10:** [1 ch, 1 tr] 4 times in ch closing 4 tr tog, sk [4 tr tog, 3 ch] ss in next sc. 1 flower made.
Fasten off A. Join B to center 1-ch sp at top of last row. Continue in rounds.
**Round 1:** 3 ch, 1 sc in same 1-ch sp, * 16 sc along side edge, [1 sc, 2 ch, 1 sc] in same place at corner, * rep from * to * twice more, 16 sc along side edge to corner, ss in first of 3 ch.
18 sc on each side.
**Round 2:** Ss into 2-ch sp, 5 ch, 2 dc in same ch sp, * 1 dc in each of 18 sc, [1 dc, 2 ch, 1 dc] in 2-ch sp, 1 dc in each of 18 sc, * [2 dc, 2 ch, 2 dc] in 2-ch sp at lower corner; rep from * to * once more, 1 dc in first 2-ch sp, ss in 3rd of 5 ch.
21 dc on each side.
Fasten off B.

## 41 KINGCUP DIAMOND
*directory view page 34*

A B

**Skill level:** intermediate
**Method of working:**
in the round

**Key:**

⌒ *Chain*

• *Slip stitch*

+ *Single*

† *Double*

‡ *Back-raised double in stitch below*

) *Back-raised treble in stitch below*

⊕ *Bobble of 3 trebles together*

↰ *Turn over*

▷ *Start/join in new color*

◀ *Fasten off*

## METHOD

**Special abbreviation**
**brtr (back raised treble):** inserting hook from back, work 1 tr around post of given stitch.

Using A, make 4 ch, join into a ring with ss in first ch.
**Round 1:** 5 ch, [1 dc into circle, 2 ch] 7 times, ss in 3$^{rd}$ of 5 ch. 24 sts.
**Round 2:** 2 ch, 2 tr tog into same place as base of these 2 ch, [2 sc in 2-ch sp, bobble of 3 tr tog in next dc] 7 times, 2 sc in last 2-ch sp, ss in top of 2 tr tog.
Fasten off A. Turn flower over so bobbles are facing. Join B from behind to stem of any dc of round 1. Work round 3 into dc of round 1, leaving round 2 at the front.
**Round 3:** 7 ch, 1 brtr in same dc, * 3 ch, 1 brtr in next dc of round 1, 3 ch, [1 brtr; 3 ch, 1 brtr] in next dc, * rep from * to * twice more, 3 ch, 1 brtr in next dc, 3 ch, ss in 4$^{th}$ of 7 ch. Twelve 3-ch sps.
**Round 4:** Ss into 3-ch sp, 7 ch, 1 tr in same ch sp, * 5 ch, 1 sc in next 3-ch sp, 3 ch, 1 sc in next ch sp, 3 ch, [1 dc, 3 ch, 1 dc] in next 3-ch sp, [3 ch, 1 sc in next 3-ch sp] twice, 5 ch, * [1 tr; 3 ch, 1 tr] in next 3-ch sp, rep from * to * once more, ss in 4$^{th}$ of 7 ch.

**Round 5:** Ss into 3-ch sp, 7 ch, 1 tr in same ch sp, * 5 ch, 1 sc in 5-ch sp, 5 dc in next 3-ch sp, 1 sc in next 3-ch sp, 3 ch, [1 dc, 3 ch, 1 dc] in next 3-ch sp, 3 ch, 1 sc in next 3-ch sp, 5 dc in next 3-ch sp, 1 sc in 5-ch sp, 5 ch, * [1 tr; 3 ch, 1 tr] in next 3-ch sp, rep from * to * once more, ss in 4$^{th}$ of 7 ch.
**Round 6:** Ss into 3-ch sp, 7 ch, 1 tr in same sp, * 5 ch, 1 sc in next 5-ch sp, 5 dc in next 3-ch sp, 1 sc in 3$^{rd}$ of 5 dc, 5 ch, 1 sc in next 3-ch sp, 3 ch, [1 dc, 3 ch, 1 dc] in next 3-ch sp, 3 ch, 1 sc in next 3-ch sp, 5 ch, 1 sc in 3$^{rd}$ of 5 dc, 5 ch, 1 sc in next 5-ch sp, 5 ch, * [1 tr; 3 ch, 1 tr] in next 3-ch sp, rep from * to * once more, ss in 4$^{th}$ of 7 ch.
**Round 7:** Ss into 3-ch sp, 3 ch, 2 sc in same sp, * [5 sc in 5-ch sp] 3 times, 3 sc in 3-ch sp, [1 sc, 2 ch, 1 sc] in next 3-ch sp, 3 sc in next 3-ch sp, [5 sc in 5-ch sp] 3 times, * [2 sc, 3 ch, 2 sc] in next 3-ch sp, rep from * to * once more, 1 sc in first ch sp of round, ss in first of 3 ch. 21 sc on each side.
Fasten off B.

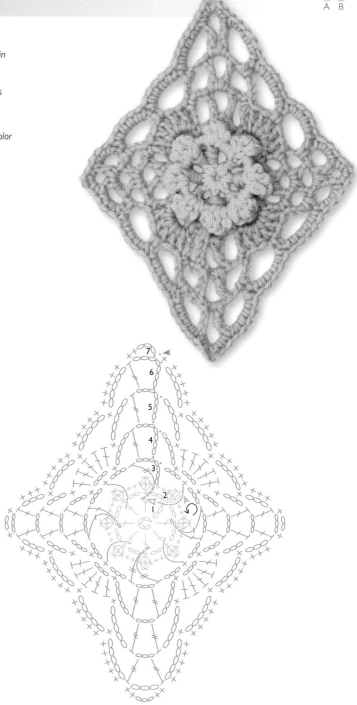

# 42 IRISH DIAMOND

*directory view page 48*

**Skill level:** easy
**Method of working:**
in the round

**Key:**

○ *Fingerwrap*

⌒ *Chain*

• *Slip stitch*

+ *Single*

◄ *Fasten off*

## METHOD

Make a fingerwrap.
**Round 1:** 1 ch, 15 sc into wrap, ss in first ch. Pull firmly on the yarn tail to make a neat circle.
**Round 2:** 1 ch, * 8 ch, sk 3 sc, 1 sc in next sc, * rep from * to * twice more, 8 ch, sk 3 sc, ss in first ch of round. 4 petals.
**Round 3:** 1 ch, * 13 sc in 8-ch loop, 1 sc in same place as next sc, * rep from * to * 3 more times.
**Round 4:** 1 ch, ss in first of 13 sc, * [1 sc in next sc, 2 ch] 10 times, 1 sc in next sc, 2 sc tog over [next and foll alt sc], * rep from * to * 3 more times, working last 2 sc tog over (next sc and ss at beg of round].
**Round 5:** 1 ch, * 7 ch, sk 9 sts, 1 sc in next sc, 7 ch, sk 11 sts, 1 sc in next sc, 7 ch, sk 9 sts, 1 sc in 2 sc tog, * rep from * to * 3 more times omitting last sc of final repeat, ss in first ch of round. 12 loops.
**Round 6:** Ss in each of next 4 ch, * 7 ch, [1 sc, 11 ch, 1 sc] in next loop (at end of petal), [7 ch, 1 sc in next loop] 5 times, * rep from * to * once more, ending in same loop as beg of round. 14 loops.

**Round 7:** Ss in each of next 4 ch, * 7 ch, [1 sc, 11 ch, 1 sc] in 11-ch loop, [7 ch, 1 sc in next loop] 6 times, * rep from * to * once more, ending in same loop as beg of round. 16 loops.
**Round 8:** Ss in each of next 4 ch, * 7 ch, 1 sc in 11-ch loop, 7 ch, ss in last sc (a large picot made), [7 ch, 1 sc in next loop] twice, 3 ch, ss in last sc (a small picot made), [7 ch, 1 sc in next loop] twice, 5 ch, ss in last sc (a medium picot made), [7 ch, 1 sc in next loop] twice, 3 ch, ss in last sc, 7 ch, 1 sc in next loop, * rep from * to * once more, ending in same loop as beg of round. Fasten off.

Blocks may be joined using the joining with picots method, page 21.

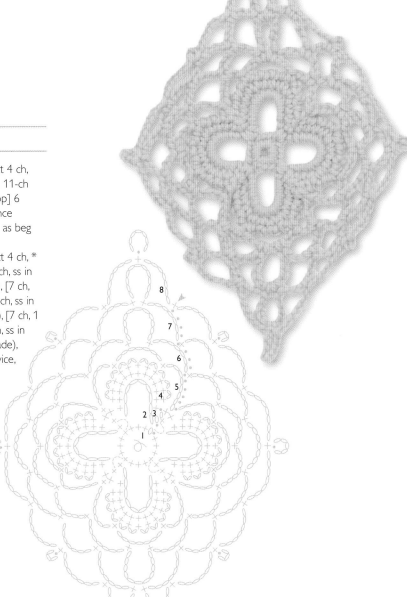

## 43 CLEMATIS DIAMOND
*directory view page 38*

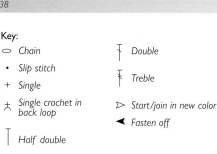

A B C

**Skill level:** easy
**Method of working:**
in the round

**Key:**

⌒ *Chain*

• *Slip stitch*

+ *Single*

⅄ *Single crochet in back loop*

丅 *Half double*

丅 *Double*

⅊ *Treble*

▷ *Start/join in new color*

◄ *Fasten off*

## METHOD

**Special abbreviation**
**bl: back loop**

Using A, make 4 ch, join into a ring with ss in first ch.
**Round 1:** 1 ch, 7 sc into ring, ss in first ch. 8 sts.
Fasten off A. Join B to bl of any sc.
**Round 2:** 1 ch, * 1 sc in bl of next sc, 10 ch, ss in 10th ch from hook, 1 sc in bl of next sc, * rep from * to * 3 more times omitting last sc of final rep, ss in first ch of round. 4 petals.
**Round 3:** 1 ch, * [2 sc, 2 hdc, 2 dc, 1 tr, 2 dc, 2 hdc, 2 sc] in 10-ch loop, sk 1 sc, 1 sc in next sc, * rep from * to * 3 more times omitting final sc, ss in first ch of round. Fasten off B. Join C to bl of tr at tip of any petal.
**Round 4:** 6 ch, 1 sc in same place, * 3 ch, [1 tr, 1 ch, 1 tr, 1 ch, 1 tr] in next sc between petals, 3 ch, # [1 sc, 5 ch, 1 sc] in bl of tr at tip of next petal, * rep from * to * twice more, then once again from * to #, ss in first of 6 ch.
**Round 5:** Ss in each of next 2 ch, ss in rem 3-ch loop, 6 ch, 1 sc in same place, * 5 ch, 1 sc in next 3-ch sp, 5 ch, sk [1 tr, 1 ch, 1 tr, 1 ch, 1 tr], 1 sc in next 3-ch sp, 5 ch, * 1 sc in 5-ch loop at tip of 2nd

petal, rep once more from * to *, [1 sc, 5 ch, 1 sc] in 5-ch loop at tip of 3rd petal, rep once more from * to *, 1 sc in 5-ch loop at tip of 4th petal, rep once more from * to *, ss in first of 6 ch.
**Round 6:** Ss in each of next 2 ch, ss in rem 3-ch loop, 6 ch, 2 dc in same place, * [5 dc in 5-ch sp] 3 times, [1 dc, 2 ch, 1 dc] in next sc (at tip of next petal), [5 dc in 5-ch sp] 3 times, * [2 dc, 3 ch, 2 dc] in next 5-ch loop (at tip of 3rd petal), rep from * to * once more, 1 dc in first loop of round 5, ss in 3rd of 6 ch.
**Round 7:** Ss into 3-ch sp, 6 ch, 2 dc in same place, * 1 dc in each of 18 dc, [1 dc, 2 ch, 1 dc] in 2-ch sp, 1 dc in each of 18 dc, * [2 dc, 3 ch, 2 dc] in 3-ch sp, rep from * to * once more, 1 dc in first ch sp, ss in 3rd of 6 ch. 21 sts on each side.
Fasten off C.

**FOUR DAISY DIAMOND**
*directory view page 40*

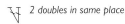
A B C D E

**Skill level:** easy
**Method of working:**
diamond in rows,
daisies in rounds

**Key:**
⬭ Chain
🇹 Double
🇦 2 doubles together
🇻 2 doubles in same place
▷ Start/join in new color
◀ Fasten off

## METHOD

### DIAMOND

Using A, make 23 ch.
**Row 1:** 2 dc tog over 4$^{th}$ and
5$^{th}$ ch from hook, 1 dc in each of
16 ch, 2 dc in next ch, 1 dc in last
ch. 21 sts.
**Row 2:** 3 ch, sk 1 dc, 2 dc in next
dc, 1 dc in each dc to last 3 sts,
2 dc tog over next 2 sts, 1 dc in
3$^{rd}$ of 3 ch.
**Row 3:** 3 ch, sk 1 dc, 2 dc tog over
next 2 sts, 1 dc in each of 2 dc,
2 ch, sk 2 dc, 1 dc in each of 8 dc,
2 ch, sk 2 dc, 1 dc in each of 2 dc,
2 dc in next dc, 1 dc in 3$^{rd}$ of 3 ch.
**Row 4:** As row 2, working 2 dc in
each 2-ch sp.
**Row 5:** 3 ch, sk 1 dc, 2 dc tog over
next 2 sts, 1 dc in each dc to last
2 sts, 2 dc in last dc, 1 dc in 3$^{rd}$
of 3 ch.
**Row 6:** As row 2.
**Row 7:** As row 5.
**Row 8:** 3 ch, sk 1 dc, 2 dc in next
dc, 1 dc in each of 2 dc, 2 ch, sk
2 dc, 1 dc in each of 8 dc, 2 ch, sk
2 dc, 1 dc in each of 2 dc, 2 dc tog
over next 2 sts, 1 dc in 3$^{rd}$ of 3 ch.

**Row 9:** As row 5, working 2 dc in
each 2-ch sp.
**Row 10:** As row 2.
Fasten off A.

### DAISIES

Using colors B, C, D, and E, work
1 daisy around each hole.
**Round 1:** With RS facing, join yarn
to first of 2 skipped dc at lower
edge of hole, 1 ch, 1 sc in next
dc, 1 sc in corner, 2 sc in dc at left
edge of hole, 1 sc in corner, 1 sc in
base of each of 2 dc at top of hole,
1 sc in corner, 2 sc in dc at right
edge of hole, 1 sc in corner, ss in
first ch. 12 sts.
**Round 2:** 6 ch, [ss in next sc, 6 ch]
11 times, ss in last ss of round 1.
Fasten off.

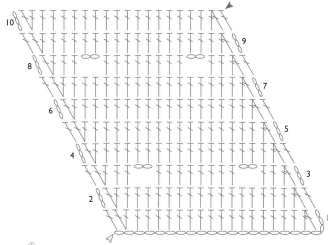

## 45 ASTER DIAMOND
*directory view page 43*

A B C D E

**Skill level:** easy
**Method of working:**
in the round

**Key:**
⌒ *Chain*

• *Slip stitch*

+ *Single*

┃ *Double*

▷ *Start/join in new color*

◄ *Fasten off*

## METHOD

### FIRST FLOWER
Using A, 10 ch, 1 sc in first ch, [9 ch, 1 sc in side of last sc] 5 times. Six 9-ch loops.
Fasten off. Sew last sc to first ch.

### SECOND FLOWER
Using B, work as first flower to last ch loop, 4 ch, ss in 9-ch loop of first flower, 4 ch, 1 sc in side of last sc.
Fasten off. Sew last sc to first ch.

### REMAINING FLOWERS
Make 3rd flower in C, joining to first and 2nd flowers as shown on chart.
Make 4th flower in D, joining to 2nd and 3rd flowers as shown.

### OUTER EDGE
With RS facing, join E to 2nd of 3 empty 9-ch loops on any flower.
**Round 1:** 5 ch, 1 sc in next 9-ch loop, [4 ch, 1 sc in next empty 9-ch loop] 12 times, 4 ch, ss in first of 5 ch. Fourteen 4-ch sps.
**Round 2:** 5 ch, 1 dc in same place, * [4 dc in 4-ch sp, 1 dc in sc] 3 times, [2 dc, 3 ch, 2 dc] in next 4-ch sp, 1 dc in next sc, [4 dc in 4-ch sp, 1 dc in sc] twice, 4 dc in 4-ch sp, * [1 dc, 2 ch, 1 dc] in next sc, rep from * to * once more, ss in 3rd of 5 ch. 18 dc in each side.
**Round 3:** Ss into 2-ch sp, 3 ch, 1 sc in same ch sp, * 1 sc in each of 18 dc, [2 sc, 3 ch, 2 sc] in 3-ch sp, 1 sc in each of 18 dc, * [1 sc, 2 ch, 1 sc] in 2-ch sp, rep from * to * once more, ss in first of 3 ch. 21 sc on each side.
Fasten off E.

# 46 COLORWORK HEXAGON
*directory view page 42*

A  B

**Skill level:** intermediate
**Method of working:**
in the round

**Key:**
⊂ *Chain*
· *Slip stitch*
+ *Single*
⋏ *2 singles together*
▷ *Start/join in new color*
◄ *Fasten off*

## METHOD

**Special abbreviation**
**chg to A (or B):** changing to A (or B) for the final "yrh, pull through" of the last st worked.

Using A, make 4 ch, join into a ring with ss in first ch.
**Round 1:** 1 ch, 5 sc into ring, ss in first ch. 6 sts.
**Round 2:** 1 ch, 2 sc in each of 5 sc, 1 sc in same place as first ch, ss in first ch. 12 sts.
**Round 3:** 1 ch, [1 sc in next sc, 2 sc in foll sc] 5 times, 1 sc in same place as first ch, ss in first ch. 18 sts. Fasten off A. Join B to any sc.
**Round 4:** 1 ch, 1 sc in each of 2 sc, [2 ch, 1 sc in each of 3 sc] 5 times, 2 ch, ss in first ch. 3 sc on each side.
**Round 5:** 1 ch, 1 sc in each sc to 2-ch sp, [1 sc in 2-ch sp, 2 ch, 1 sc in each sc to 2-ch sp] 5 times, 1 sc in 2-ch sp, 2 ch, ss in first ch. 4 sc on each side.
**Rounds 6–8:** As round 5. 7 sc on each side.
**Round 9:** 1 ch, 1 sc in each of 6 sc, * chg to A, 1 sc in 2-ch sp, 2 ch, chg to B, # 1 sc in each of 7 sc, * rep from * to * 4 more times, then once again from * to #, ss in first ch. 8 sc on each side.
On rounds 9–14, enclose color not in use by working over it until it is required.
**Round 10:** 1 ch, 1 sc in each of 5 sc, * chg to A, 1 sc in each of 2 sc, 1 sc in 2-ch sp, 2 ch, chg to B,

# 1 sc in each of 6 sc, * rep from * to * 4 more times, then once again from * to #, ss in first ch. 9 sc on each side.
**Round 11:** 1 ch, 1 sc in each of 4 sc, * chg to A, 1 sc in each of 4 sc, 1 sc in 2-ch sp, 2 ch, chg to B, # 1 sc in each of 5 sc, * rep from * to * 4 more times, then once again from * to #, ss in first ch. 10 sc on each side.
**Round 12:** 1 ch, 1 sc in each of 3 sc, * chg to A, 1 sc in each of 6 sc, 1 sc in 2-ch sp, 2 ch, chg to B, # 1 sc in each of 4 sc, * rep from * to * 4 more times, then once again from * to #, ss in first ch. 11 sc on each side.
**Round 13:** 1 ch, 1 sc in each of 2 sc, * chg to A, 1 sc in each of 8 sc, 1 sc in 2-ch sp, 2 ch, chg to B, # 1 sc in each of 3 sc, * rep from * to * 4 more times, then once again from * to #, ss in first ch. 12 sc on each side.
**Round 14:** 1 ch, 1 sc in next sc, * chg to A, 1 sc in each of 10 sc, 1 sc in 2-ch sp, 2 ch, chg to B, # 1 sc in each of 2 sc, * rep from * to * 4 more times, then once again from * to #, ss in first ch. 13 sc on each side.
Fasten off B. Continue in A.
**Rounds 15–16:** As round 5. 15 sc on each side.
Fasten off A.

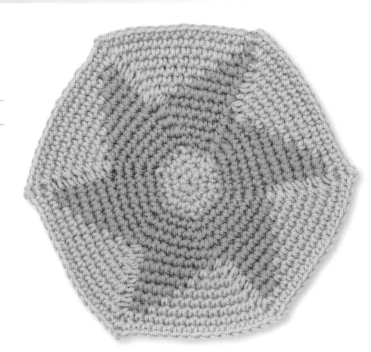

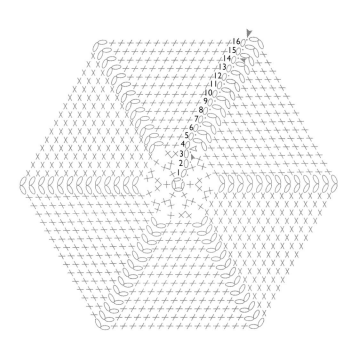

## 47 LARGE FLOWER HEXAGON
*directory view page 39*

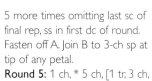
A  B

**Skill level:** intermediate
**Method of working:** in the round

**Key:**
⌒ *Chain*
• *Slip stitch*
+ *Single*
† *Double*
‡ *Treble*

⅄ *2 trebles together*
▷ *Start/join in new color*
◄ *Fasten off*

## METHOD

Using A, make 8 ch, join into a ring with ss in first ch.

**Round 1:** 3 ch, 1 tr into ring, [2 ch, 2 tr tog into ring] 11 times, 2 ch, ss in first tr of round.

**Round 2:** Ss into 2-ch sp, 1 ch, [5 ch, 1 sc in next 2-ch sp] 11 times, 5 ch, ss in first ch of round.

**Round 3:** Ss into each of 2 ch, 1 ch, * 10 ch, 1 sc in same 5-ch sp, [5 ch, 1 sc in next 5-ch sp] # twice, * rep from * to * 4 more times, then once again from * to #, 2 ch, 1 dc in first ch of round.

**Round 4:** * [5 dc, 3 ch, 5 dc] in 10-ch loop, 1 sc in next 5-ch sp, [2 dc, 1 ch, 2 dc] in next sc, 1 sc in next 5-ch sp, * rep from * to *

5 more times omitting last sc of final rep, ss in first dc of round. Fasten off A. Join B to 3-ch sp at tip of any petal.

**Round 5:** 1 ch, * 5 ch, [1 tr, 3 ch, 1 tr] in next 1-ch sp, 5 ch, 1 sc in next 3-ch sp, * rep from * to * 5 more times omitting last sc of final rep, ss in first ch of round.

**Round 6:** Ss into 5-ch sp, 1 ch, 4 sc in same sp, * 1 sc in tr, 3 sc in 3-ch sp, 1 sc in tr, 5 sc in 5-ch sp, 2 ch, sk 1 sc, # 5 sc in 5-ch sp, * rep from * to * 4 more times, then once again from * to #, ss in first ch of round. 15 sts on each side. Fasten off B.

**MIX AND MATCH: 47 + 48**

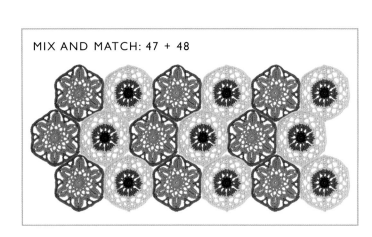

# 48 CORNFLOWER HEXAGON
*directory view page 39*

A B C

**Skill level:** intermediate
**Method of working:**
in the round

**Key:**

◦ *Chain*

• *Slip stitch*

+ *Single*

┬ *Double*

⚇ *Treble*

⋎ *Petal (as special abbreviation)*

▷ *Start/join in new color*

◀ *Fasten off*

## METHOD

**Special abbreviation**

**petal:** 1 dtr in position as given, [1 tr in side of this dtr; inserting hook under 2 threads of 2$^{nd}$ node from base] twice.

Using A, make 6 ch, join into a ring with ss in first ch.
**Round 1:** 3 ch, [1 sc into ring, 2 ch] 11 times, 2 ch, ss in first of 3 ch. Fasten off A. Join B to any 2-ch sp.
**Round 2:** 5 ch, 2 tr in 4$^{th}$ ch from hook, [1 ch, 1 petal in next 2-ch sp] 11 times, 1 ch, ss in 5$^{th}$ of 5 ch. Fasten off B. Join C to any 1-ch sp.
**Round 3:** 3 ch, 1 sc in same ch sp, * [1 sc between next 2 sts] twice, 1 sc in next 1-ch sp, [1 sc between next 2 sts] twice, # [1 sc, 2 ch, 1 sc] in next 1-ch sp, * rep from * to * 4 more times, then once again from * to #, ss in first of 3 ch.
**Round 4:** Ss into 2-ch sp, 5 ch, 1 dc in same ch sp, * 5 ch, sk 3 sc, 1 sc in next sc, 5 ch, sk 3 sc, # [1 dc, 2 ch, 1 dc] in 2-ch sp, * rep from * to * 4 more times, then once again from * to #, ss in 3$^{rd}$ of 5 ch.

**Round 5:** Ss into 2-ch sp, 5 ch, 1 dc in same ch sp, * 3 ch, 1 sc in next 5-ch sp, 6 ch, 1 sc in next 5-ch sp, 3 ch, # [1 dc, 2 ch, 1 dc] in 2-ch sp, * rep from * to * 4 more times, then once again from * to #, ss in 3$^{rd}$ of 5 ch.
**Round 6:** Ss into 2-ch sp, 3 ch, 1 sc in same ch sp, * 1 sc in 3-ch sp, 2 ch, 1 dc in next sc, 2 ch, 1 sc in 6-ch sp, 2 ch, 1 dc in next sc, 2 ch, 1 sc in 3-ch sp, # [1 sc, 2 ch, 1 sc] in 2-ch sp, * rep from * to * 4 more times, then once again from * to #, ss in first of 3 ch.
**Round 7:** Ss into 2-ch sp, 3 ch, 1 sc in same ch sp, * sk 1 sc, 1 sc in next sc, [2 sc in next 2-ch sp, 1 sc in next st] 4 times, sk 1 sc, # [1 sc, 2 ch, 1 sc] in corner 2-ch sp, rep from * to * 4 more times, then once again from * to #, ss in first of 3 ch. 15 sc on each side. Fasten off C.

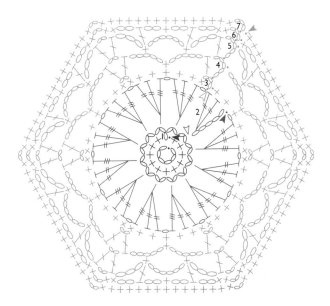

## 49 FRILLED FLOWER HEXAGON

*directory view page 42*

**Skill level:** advanced

**Method of working:** in the round

**Key:**

○ Chain

• Slip stitch

+ Single

⊥ Single in back loop

↓ Single in 2-ch space behind petal

┬ Double

┬ Double in front loop of round 1

⌃ Front-raised double

⋏ 3 front-raised doubles together

5 front-raised trebles around stem of double

Double treble in front loop of round 1

▷ Start/join in new color

◀ Fasten off

## METHOD

**Special abbreviation**

**frdc (front-raised dc):** inserting hook from front, work dc around post of st on previous row.

Using A, make 5 ch, join into a ring with ss in first ch.

**Round 1:** 1 ch, 11 sc into ring, ss into first ch. 12 sts.

**Round 2:** 1 ch, [1 sc in back loop of next sc, 2 sc in back loop of foll sc] 5 times, 1 sc in back loop of last sc, 1 sc in back loop of ch at base of 1 ch, ss in first ch of round. 18 sts.

**Round 3:** 3 ch, 1 dc in each of first 2 sc, * 1 tr in front loop of sc of round 1 below, 1 dc in each of next 3 sc of round 2, * rep from * to * 4 more times, 1 tr in front loop of sc of round 1 below, ss in 3rd of 3 ch.

**Round 4:** 3 ch, 1 dc in each of 2 dc, * [1 dc, 2 ch, 1 dc] in tr, 1 dc in each of 3 dc, * rep from * to * 4 more times, [1 dc, 2 ch, 1 dc] in tr, ss in 3rd of 3 ch.

**Round 5:** 1 ch, 1 sc in each of 3 dc, * working in front of 2 ch, 5 tr around stem of tr of round 3 below, 1 sc in each of 5 dc, *

rep from * to * 4 more times, 5 tr around stem of tr of round 3 below, 1 sc in next dc, ss in first ch. Fasten off A. Join B to first tr of any group of 5 tr.

**Round 6:** * [4 ch, ss in next tr] 4 times, 1 dtr in empty front loop of sc of round 1 below, ss in next tr, * rep from * to * 5 more times working final ss in same place as first ss of round. Fasten off B. Join C to any dtr.

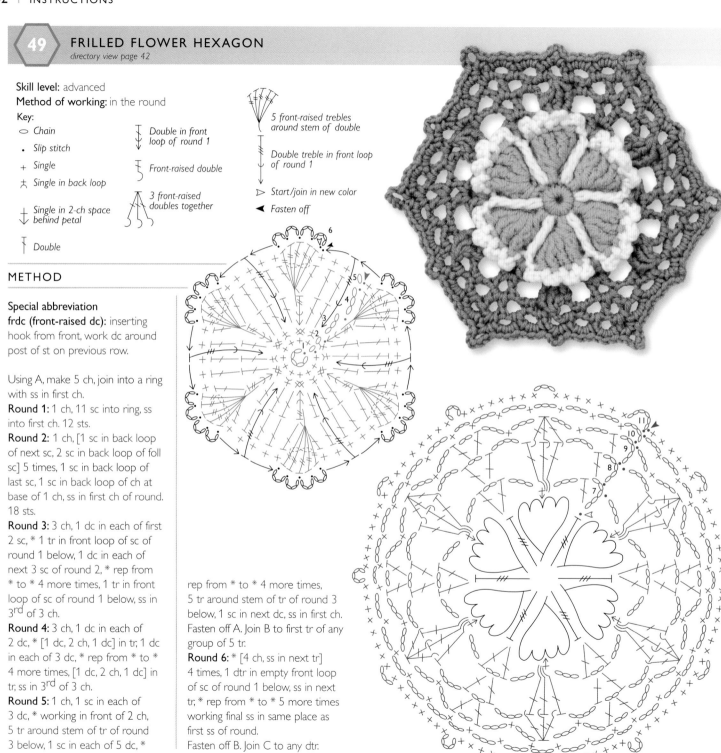

**Round 7:** 5 ch, 1 dc in same dtr, * 3 ch, 1 sc in 2-ch sp behind petal, 3 ch, [1 dc, 2 ch, 1 dc] in next dtr, * rep from * to * 4 more times, 3 ch, 1 sc in 2-ch sp behind petal, 3 ch, ss in 3rd of 5 ch.
**Round 8:** Ss into 2-ch sp, 5 ch, 1 dc in same ch sp, * 4 ch, 3 frdc in next sc, 4 ch, [1 dc, 2 ch, 1 dc] in next 2-ch sp, * rep from * to * 4 more times, 4 ch, 3 frdc in next sc, 4 ch, ss in 3rd of 5 ch.
**Round 9:** Ss into 2-ch sp, 5 ch, 1 dc in same ch sp, * 3 ch, 1 sc in 4-ch sp, 3 ch, 3 frdc tog over next 3 frdc, 3 ch, 1 sc in 4-ch sp, 3 ch, [1 dc, 2 ch, 1 dc] in 2-ch sp, * rep from * to * 4 more times, 3 ch, 1 sc in 4-ch sp, 3 ch, 3 frdc tog over next 3 frdc, 3 ch, 1 sc in 4-ch sp, 3 ch, ss in 3rd of 5 ch.
**Round 10:** Ss into 2-ch sp, 4 ch, 1 sc in same ch sp, * [3 ch, 1 sc in next 3-ch sp] 4 times, 3 ch, [1 sc, 3 ch, 1 sc] in 2-ch sp, * rep from * to * 4 more times, [3 ch, 1 sc in next 3-ch sp] 4 times, 3 ch, ss in first ch.
**Round 11:** Ss into 3-ch sp, 6 ch, * [3 sc in next 3-ch sp] twice, [1 sc, 3 ch, 1 sc] in next 3-ch sp, [3 sc in next 3-ch sp] twice, [1 sc, 5 ch, 1 sc] in 3-ch sp at corner, * rep from * to * 4 more times, [3 sc in next 3-ch sp] twice, [1 sc, 3 ch, 1 sc] in next 3-ch sp, [3 sc in next 3-ch sp] twice, ss in first of 6 ch.
Fasten off C.

Blocks may be joined using the joining with picots method, page 21.

**Skill level:** intermediate
**Method of working:** in the round

**Key:**

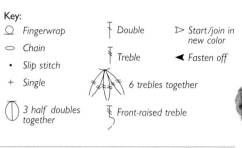

○ *Fingerwrap*  ⊤ *Double*  ▷ *Start/join in new color*
⌒ *Chain*  ⊤ *Treble*  ◀ *Fasten off*
• *Slip stitch*
+ *Single*  ⋀ *6 trebles together*
⋃ *3 half doubles together*  ⊤ *Front-raised treble*

## METHOD

**Special abbreviation**
**frtr (front-raised tr):** inserting hook from front, work tr around post of st on previous row.

Using A, make a fingerwrap.
**Round 1:** 4 ch, [2 dc into wrap, 1 ch, 1 dc into wrap, 1 ch] 5 times, 2 dc into wrap, 1 ch, ss in 3rd of 4 ch. 24 sts.
**Round 2:** 6 ch, [1 tr in each of 2 dc, 2 ch, 1 tr in next dc, 2 ch] 5 times, 1 tr in each of 2 dc, 2 ch, ss in 4th of 6 ch. 42 sts.
**Round 3:** 7 ch, [1 frtr in each of 2 tr, 4 ch, 1 dc in next tr, 4 ch] 5 times, 1 frtr in each of 2 tr, 4 ch, ss in 3rd of 7 ch. 66 sts.
Fasten off A. Join B to 2nd of 4 ch following any 2 frtr.
**Round 4:** 3 ch, 5 tr tog inserting hook [once in same place as base of 3 ch, twice in next dc, twice in foll 3rd ch], * 13 ch, sk 2 frtr; 6 tr tog inserting hook [twice in 2nd of 4 ch, twice in next dc, twice in foll 3rd ch], * rep from * to * 4 more times, 13 ch, ss in ch closing first 5 tr tog.
Fasten off B. Join A to ch closing any 6 tr tog.
**Round 5:** 1 ch, 3 hdc tog in same ch, * 1 ch, 7 sc in 13-ch sp, 2 frtr tog over 2 frtr of round 3 below, 7 sc in same ch sp, 1 ch, # 3 hdc tog in ch closing next group, * rep from * to * 4 more times, then once again from * to #, ss in first 3 hdc tog. 15 sts on each side, 3 sts at each corner.
Fasten off A.

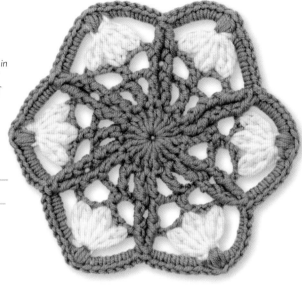

## 51 OLD FRENCH ROSE HEXAGON

*directory view page 43*

A B

**Skill level:** intermediate
**Method of working:** in the round

**Key:**
◠ Chain
• Slip stitch
+ Single
⊤ Double

▷ Start/join in new color
◀ Fasten off

## METHOD

Using A, make 9 ch, join into a ring with 1 ss in first ch.

**Round 1:** 1 ch, 17 sc into ring, ss into first ch. 18 sts.

**Round 2:** 4 ch, [sk 2 sc, 1 sc in next sc, 3 ch,] 5 times, sk 2 sc, ss in first of 4 ch. 6 ch sps.

**Round 3:** [1 sc, 3 ch, 5 dc, 3 ch, 1 sc] in each of 6 ch sps, ss in first sc.

**Round 4:** Work behind round 3: 1 ch, [5 ch, 1 sc between next 2 sc where petals adjoin] 5 times, 5 ch, ss in first ch of round.

**Round 5:** [1 sc, 3 ch, 7 tr, 3 ch, 1 sc] in each of 6 ch sps, ss in first sc. Fasten off A. Join B between any 2 petals, between 2 sc.

**Round 6:** Work behind round 5: 1 ch, [6 ch, 1 sc between next 2 sc where petals adjoin] 5 times, 6 ch, ss in first ch of round.

**Round 7:** 5 ch, 1 dc in same place as base of these 5 ch, * 7 dc in 7-ch sp, [1 dc, 2 ch, 1 dc] in next sc, * rep from * to * 4 more times, 7 dc in 7-ch sp, ss in 3$^{rd}$ of 5 ch.

**Round 8:** Ss into 2-ch sp, 5 ch, 1 dc in same ch sp, * sk 1 dc, 3 dc in next dc, [sk 2 dc, 3 dc in next dc] twice, sk 1 dc, # [1 dc, 2 ch, 1 dc] in 2-ch sp, * rep from * to * 4 more times, then once again from * to #, ss in 3$^{rd}$ of 5 ch.

**Round 9:** Ss back between previous dc and 3 ch, 5 ch, * sk 1 dc, 3 dc in sp between 2 groups, [sk 3 dc, 3 dc in space between 2 groups] 3 times, # 2 ch, sk [1 dc, 2 ch, 1 dc], * rep from * to * 4 more times, then once again from * to # omitting final dc of last repeat, ss in 3$^{rd}$ of 5 ch.

**Round 10:** Ss into 3-ch sp, 5 ch, 3 dc in same ch sp, * [sk 3 dc, 3 dc in space between 2 groups] 3 times, # sk 3 dc, [3 dc, 2 ch, 3 dc] in 2-ch sp, * rep from * to * 4 more times, then once again from * to #, sk last group, 2 dc in first ch sp, ss in 3$^{rd}$ of 5 ch.

Fasten off B.

# 52 DIANTHUS HEXAGON
*directory view page 47*

A B C

**Skill level:** intermediate
**Method of working:**
in the round

**Key:**
Ω *Fingerwrap*
⌒ *Chain*
• *Slip stitch*
+ *Single*
T *Half double*

T *Double*
Ŧ *Treble*
▷ *Start/join in new color*
◄ *Fasten off*

## METHOD

Using A, make a fingerwrap.
**Round 1:** 2 ch, 8 hdc into wrap, ss in 2$^{nd}$ of 2 ch. 9 sts.
Join in B, leaving A at back of work.
**Round 2:** Using B, 1 ch, 2 sc in each hdc, 1 sc in same place as first ch of round, ss in first ch. 18 sts. Change to A, leaving B at back of work.
**Round 3:** Using A, * 3 ch, [2 tr in next sc] twice, 3 ch, ss in next sc, * rep from * to * 5 more times, ending in same sc as beg of round. Fasten off A.
**Round 4:** Using B, 3 ch, * ss in 3$^{rd}$ of 3 ch of round 3, [2 ch, ss in next tr] 4 times, 2 ch, ss in next ch, 1 dc in same place as ss of round 3 below, * rep from * to * omitting last dc of final repeat, ss in 3$^{rd}$ of 3 ch at beg of round.
Fasten off B. Join C to any dc.
**Round 5:** 1 ch, * 5 ch, sk [ss, 2 ch, ss, 2 ch, ss], ss in back loop of next ch, 5 ch, sk [1 ch, ss, 2 ch, ss, 2 ch, ss], 1 sc in next dc, * rep from * to * 5 more times omitting last sc of final repeat, ss in first ch of round.

**Round 6:** 6 ch, 1 sc in next 5-ch loop, * 5 ch, 1 sc in next 5-ch loop, 3 ch, 1 dc in next sc, 3 ch, 1 sc in next 5-ch loop, * rep from * to * 4 more times, 5 ch, 1 sc in next 5-ch loop, 3 ch, ss in 3$^{rd}$ of 6 ch.
**Round 7:** 6 ch, 1 sc in next loop, * [5 ch, 1 sc in next loop] twice, 3 ch, 1 dc in next dc, 3 ch, 1 sc in next loop, * rep from * to * 4 more times, [5 ch, 1 sc in next loop] twice, 3 ch, ss in 3$^{rd}$ of 6 ch.
**Round 8:** 6 ch, ss in 4$^{th}$ ch from hook (a 3-ch picot made), * 3 ch, 1 sc in next loop, [5 ch, 1 sc in next loop] 3 times, 3 ch, 1 dc in next dc, 3 ch, ss in top of dc just made, * rep from * to * omitting last dc and picot of final repeat, ss in same ch as base of first picot. Fasten off C.

Blocks can be joined using the joining with picots method (see page 21).

## 53 SPIRAL WINDFLOWER HEXAGON
*directory view page 41*

A B C

**Skill level:** easy
**Method of working:**
in the round

**Key:**
- ◯ *Chain*
- • *Slip stitch*
- + *Single*
- ⊤ *Treble*
- ▷ *Start/join in new color*
- ◀ *Fasten off*

## METHOD

Using A, make 6 ch, join into a ring with ss in first ch.
**Round 1:** 1 ch, 11 sc into ring, ss in first ch. 12 sts.
Fasten off A. Join B to any sc.
**Round 2:** 1 ch, * 3 ch, [1 tr, 1 ch, 1 tr] in next sc, 3 ch, 1 sc in next sc, * rep from * to * 5 more times omitting last sc of final repeat, ss in first ch of round. 6 petals made.
Fasten off B. Join C to 1-ch sp at top of any petal.
**Round 3:** 1 ch, * 6 ch, 1 sc in 1-ch sp at top of next petal, * rep from * to * 4 more times, 6 ch, ss in first ch of round.
**Round 4:** * 4 ch, 3 sc in 6-ch sp, 1 sc in sc, * rep from * to * 5 more times working last sc in first ch.

**Round 5:** * 4 ch, 2 sc in 4-ch sp, 1 sc in each of 3 sc, sk 1 sc, * rep from * to * 5 more times.
**Round 6:** * 4 ch, 2 sc in 4-ch sp, 1 sc in each sc to last sc of group, sk 1 sc, * rep from * to * 5 more times.
Rep round 6 six more times, until there are 4 ch and 12 sc on each side of hexagon, ss into next sc.
Fasten off C.
(Note: It is easy to adjust the size of this hexagon by repeating round 6 to any size required.)

**DAFFODIL HEXAGON**
*directory view page 32*

A  B  C

**Skill level:** easy
**Method of working:** in the round

**Key:**
○ *Chain*
• *Slip stitch*
+ *Single*
⊥ *Single in front loop*
⋎ *2 singles in same front loop*
T *Double*

*3 double trebles together in back loops of round 1*

▷ *Start/join in new color*
◄ *Fasten off*

## METHOD

**Special abbreviation**
**3-ch P (3-ch picot):** 3 ch, ss in top of previous st.

Using A, make 5 ch, join into a ring with ss in first ch.
**Round 1:** 1 ch, 11 sc into ring, ss in first ch. 12 sts.
**Round 2:** 1 ch, [2 sc in front loop of next sc, 1 sc in front loop of next sc] 5 times, 2 sc in front loop of last sc, ss in first ch. 18 sts. Fasten off A. Join B to back loop of any sc of round 1 that contains 2 sc.
**Round 3:** Work in back loops of round 1: * 3 ch, 3 dtr tog over [same loop and next 2 back loops], 3-ch P, 4 ch, ss in same back loop, * rep from * to * 5 more times ending in same loop as beg of round. 6 petals.
Fasten off B. Join C to any 3-ch P.
**Round 4:** 1 ch, * 4 ch, 1 dtr in ss between two petals, 4 ch, 1 sc in next 3-ch P, * rep from * to * 5 more times omitting final sc, ss in first ch. 12 ch sps.

**Round 5:** 5 ch, 1 dc in same place, * 4 dc in 4-ch sp, 1 dc in sc, 4 dc in 4-ch sp, [1 dc, 2 ch, 1 dc] in 2-ch sp, * rep from * to * 4 more times, 4 dc in 4-ch sp, 1 dc in sc, 4 dc in 4-ch sp, ss in 3rd of 5 ch. 11 dc on each side.
**Round 6:** Ss into 2-ch sp, 5 ch, 1 dc in same ch sp, * [1 ch, sk 1 dc, 1 dc in next dc] 5 times, 1 ch, sk 1 dc, # [1 dc, 2 ch, 1 dc] in 2-ch sp, * rep from * to * 4 more times, then once again from * to #, ss in 3rd of 5 ch.
**Round 7:** Ss into 2-ch sp, 5 ch, 1 dc in same ch sp, * 1 dc in each dc and ch sp to next corner, [1 dc, 2 ch, 1 dc] in 2-ch sp, * rep from * to * 4 more times, 1 dc in each dc and ch sp, ss in 3rd of 5 ch. 15 dc on each side.
Fasten off C.

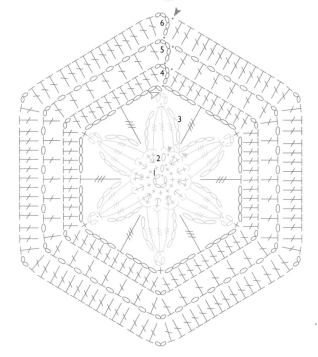

## 55 BUSY LIZZIE HEXAGON
*directory view page 44*

A B C

**Skill level:** intermediate
**Method of working:** in the round

**Key:**

Ω  *Fingerwrap*

◡  *Chain*

•  *Slip stitch*

+  *Single*

⋏  *2 singles together*

⬭  *3 trebles together*

▷  *Start/join in new color*

◀  *Fasten off*

## METHOD

Using A, make a fingerwrap.
**Round 1:** 3 ch, 2 tr tog into wrap, [5 ch, 3 tr tog into wrap] 5 times, 5 ch, ss in top of 2 tr tog. 6 petals. Fasten off A. Join B to any 3 tr tog.
**Round 2:** 3 ch, [2 tr tog, 7 ch, 3 tr tog] in same place as base of first 3 ch, * [3 tr tog, 7 ch, 3 tr tog] in top of next 3 tr tog, * rep from * to * 4 more times, ss in top of first 2 tr tog. 6 pairs of petals.
**Round 3:** 3 ch, [2 tr tog, 5 ch, 2 tr tog] in same place as base of first 3 ch, * ss in 7-ch sp, sk 3 tr tog, [2 tr tog, 5 ch, 3 tr tog, 5 ch, 2 tr tog] in top of next 3 tr tog. * rep from * to * 4 more times, ss in 7-ch sp, 2 tr tog in same place as base of first 3 ch of round, 5 ch, ss in first 2 tr tog. 6 flowers completed.

Fasten off B. Join C to ch closing 3 tr tog at top of any flower.
**Round 4:** 3 ch, 1 sc in same place, * 5 sc in 5-ch sp, 2 sc tog over next two 2 tr tog (omitting ss between petals), 5 sc in 5-ch sp, # [1 sc, 2 ch, 1 sc] in ch closing next 3 tr tog, rep from * to * 4 more times, then once again from * to #, ss in first of 3 ch. 13 sc on each side.
**Round 5:** Ss into 2-ch sp, 3 ch, 1 sc in same ch sp, * 1 sc in each of 13 sts, [1 sc, 2 ch, 1 sc] in 2-ch sp, * rep from * to * 4 more times, 1 sc in each of 13 sts, ss in first of 3 ch. 15 sc on each side. Fasten off C.

# 56 WILD ROSE HEXAGON
*directory view page 46*

A B C D

**Skill level:** intermediate
**Method of working:** in the round

**Key:**
- ⌒ Chain
- • Slip stitch
- + Single
- ⅄ Single in back loop
- ⊤ Double
- ⌇ Back-raised double
- ⌇ Treble in front loop
- ⌇ Double treble
- ⌇ Double treble in front loop
- ◖ Popcorn of 4 half doubles in double below
- ▷ Start/join in new color
- ◀ Fasten off

## METHOD

**Special abbreviations**
**PC (4-hdc popcorn):** work as for 4-dc popcorn (page 127) but using 4 hdc.
**brdc (back raised dc):** inserting hook from back, work dc around post of st on previous row.

Using A, make 5 ch, join into a ring with ss in first ch.
**Round 1:** 3 ch, 9 dc into ring, ss in 3rd of 3 ch. 10 dc.
Fasten off A. Join B to space between any 2 dc.
**Round 2:** 3 ch, [1 brdc in next dc, 1 dc in sp before next dc] 9 times, 1 brdc in last dc, ss in 3rd of 3 ch. 20 sts.
**Round 3:** Work throughout in front loops of round 2: ss in next st, * 3 ch, 1 tr in st at base of these 3 ch, [1 tr; 1 dtr] in next st, [1 dtr; 1 tr] in next st, [1 tr, 3 ch, ss] in next st, ss in next st, * rep from * to * 4 more times working final ss in same place as first ss of round. 5 petals made.
Fasten off B. Join C to any back loop of round 2.
**Round 4:** Work in back loops of round 2: 1 ch, [2 sc in next st, 1 sc in next st] 9 times, 2 sc in last st, ss in first ch. 30 sts.
**Round 5:** 5 ch, [2 dc in next sc, 1 dc in each of 3 sc, 2 dc in next sc, 2 ch] 5 times, 2 dc in next sc, 1 dc in each

of 3 sc, 1 dc in same place as base of 5 ch, ss in 3rd of 5 ch.
7 sts on each side.
**Round 6:** Ss into 2-ch sp, 5 ch, 1 dc in same 2-ch sp, * 1 dc in each of 7 dc to 2-ch sp, [1 dc, 2 ch, 1 dc] in 2-ch sp, * rep from to * 4 more times, 1 dc in each of 7 dc, ss in 3rd of 5 ch. 9 sts on each side.
Fasten off C. Join D to any 2-ch sp.
**Round 7:** 5 ch, 1 dc in same 2-ch sp, * sk 4 dc, [1 dtr, 4 ch, ss, 4 ch, 1 dtr] in next dc, sk 4 dc, [1 dc, 2 ch, 1 dc] in 2-ch sp, * rep to * 4 more times, sk 4 dc, [1 dtr, 4 ch, ss, 4 ch, 1 dtr] in next dc, sk 4 dc, ss in 3rd of 5 ch.
Fasten off D. Join B to any 2-ch sp.
**Round 8:** 3 ch, 1 sc in same 2-ch sp, * 5 ch, sk [1 dc, 4 ch], PC in dc of round 6 below next ss, 5 ch, sk [4 ch, 1 dc], [1 sc, 2 ch, 1 sc] in 2-ch sp, * rep from * to * 4 more times, 5 ch, sk [1 dc, 4 ch], PC in dc of round 6 below next ss, 5 ch, sk [4 ch, 1 dc], ss in first of 3 ch.
Fasten off B. Join C to any 2-ch sp.
**Round 9:** 3 ch, 1 sc in same 2-ch sp, * sk 1 sc, 6 sc in 5-ch sp, 1 sc in top of PC, 6 sc in 5-ch sp, sk 1 sc, [1 sc, 2 ch, 1 sc] in 2-ch sp, * rep from * to * 4 more times, sk 1 sc, 6 sc in 5-ch sp, 1 sc in top of PC, 6 sc in 5-ch sp, sk 1 sc, ss in first of 3 ch. 15 sc on each side.
Fasten off C.

## 57 GARLAND HEXAGON
*directory view page 45*

A  B  C

**Skill level:** intermediate
**Method of working:** in the round

**Key:**
Ꭴ *Fingerwrap*
⌒ *Chain*
• *Slip stitch*
+ *Single*
Ŧ *Double*

Ŧ *Treble*

*5 double trebles together*

▷ *Start/join in new color*
◄ *Fasten off*

---

## METHOD

**FIRST FLOWER**
Using A, make a fingerwrap.
**Round 1:** 4 ch, [1 dc into wrap, 1 ch] 9 times, ss in 3rd of 4 ch. 20 sts.
**Round 2:** 4 ch, [1 sc in next dc, 3 ch, sk 1 ch] 9 times, ss in first of 4 ch. Ten 3-ch loops.
Fasten off.

**SECOND FLOWER**
Using B, work as first flower to end of round 1.
**Round 2:** 4 ch, [1 sc in next dc, 3 ch, sk 1 ch] 7 times, [1 sc in next dc, 1 ch, ss in 3-ch loop of first flower, 1 ch, sk 1 ch] twice, ss in first of 4 ch.
Fasten off.

**REMAINING FLOWERS**
Make 3rd flower in A, 4th flower in B, and 5th flower in A, joining each to previous flower at two loops as shown on chart.
Make 6th flower in B, joining to 5th and first flowers as shown, to form a circle.

**CENTER**
With RS facing, join C to any empty 3-ch loop inside circle, 5 ch, 5 dtr tog over next 5 empty 3-ch loops. Fasten off.

**OUTER EDGE**
With RS facing, join C to 3rd of 5 empty 3-ch loops on any flower.
**Round 1:** 5 ch, 1 dc in same 3-ch loop, * 1 ch, 1 sc in next 3-ch loop, 3 ch, 2 tr tog over [next 3-ch loop and first empty 3-ch loop of next flower], 3 ch, 1 sc in next 3-ch loop, 1 ch, # [1 dc, 3 ch, 1 dc] in next 3-ch loop *, rep from * to * 4 more times, then once again from * to #, ss in 3rd of 5 ch.
**Round 2:** Ss into 2-ch sp, 3 ch, 1 sc in same ch sp, * 1 sc in next dc, 1 sc in 1-ch sp, 1 sc in sc, 3 sc in 3-ch sp, 1 sc in 2 tr tog, 3 sc in 3-ch sp, 1 sc in sc, 1 sc in 1-ch sp, 1 sc in dc, # [1 sc, 2 ch, 1 sc] in 3-ch sp at corner *, rep from * to * 4 more times, then once again from * to #, ss in first of 3 ch. 15 sc on each side.
Fasten off C.

# 58 LOOPY FLOWER HEXAGON

*directory view page 46*

A  B

**Skill level:** advanced
**Method of working:** in the round

**Key:**
Ω Fingerwrap
◠ Chain
• Slip stitch
+ Single
⌔ Single in stitch below

T Double
Ŧ Front-raised double
▷ Start/join in new color
◄ Fasten off

## METHOD

**Special abbreviations**
**frdc (front-raised dc):** inserting hook from front, work dc around post of given st.

Using A, make a fingerwrap.
**Round 1:** 1 ch, 5 sc into wrap, ss in first ch. 6 sts.
**Round 2:** 5 ch, [1 dc in next sc, 2 ch] 5 times, ss in 3$^{rd}$ of 5 ch. Six 2-ch sps.
**Round 3:** Ss into 2-ch sp, * 2 ch, 1 frdc around these 2 ch, [1 frdc in previous frdc] 10 times, ss in same place as base of 2 ch, 1 sc in 2-ch sp, ss in next dc, * rep from * to * 5 more times working final ss in same place as base of first 2 ch. 6 petal loops.
Fasten off A.
**Round 4:** Using B, make 60 ch. Thread beginning of ch from front to back through 6 petal loops, working counterclockwise; without twisting, ss in first ch to make a large circle.

**Round 5:** 6 ch, [sk 1 petal loop, 9 sc into circle, 5 ch] 5 times, sk last petal loop, 8 sc into circle, ss into first of 6 ch. 9 sc on each side.
**Round 6:** Ss into 5-ch sp, 3 ch, 2 sc in same ch sp, * 9 ch, sk 9 sc, [2 sc, 2 ch, 2 sc] in 5-ch sp, * rep from * to * 4 more times, 9 ch, sk 9 sc, 1 sc in first ch sp, ss in first of 3 ch.
**Round 7:** Ss into 2-ch sp, 3 ch, 1 sc in same ch sp, * 1 sc in each of 2 sc, 3 sc in 9-ch sp, 1 sc into each of 3 center sc of round 5 below (enclosing center of 9 ch), 3 sc in same 9-ch sp, 1 sc in each of 2 sc, # [1 sc, 2 ch, 1 sc] in 2-ch sp, * rep from * to * 4 more times, then once again from * to #, ss in first of 3 ch. 15 sc on each side.
Fasten off B.

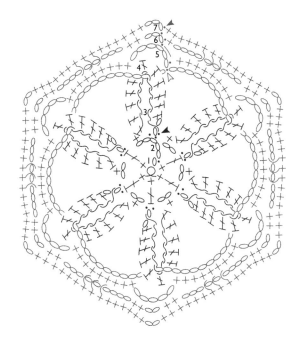

## 59 STAR FLOWER HEXAGON
*directory view page 50*

**Skill level:** easy
**Method of working:** in the round

**Key:**
⌒ *Chain*
• *Slip stitch*
+ *Single*
† *Double*
⋏ *2 doubles together*
⋏⋏ *3 doubles together*
◄ *Fasten off*

## METHOD

Make 8 ch, join into a ring with ss in first ch.

**Round 1:** 4 ch, [3 dc into ring, 1 ch] 5 times, 2 dc into ring, ss in 3rd of 4 ch.

**Round 2:** Ss into 1-ch sp, 6 ch, 1 sc in same ch sp, * 5 ch, [1 sc, 5 ch, 1 sc] in next 1-ch sp, * rep from * to * 4 more times, 5 ch, ss in first of 6 ch.

**Round 3:** Ss into next ch, ss into rem 4-ch sp, 5 ch, 1 dc in same ch sp, * 1 ch, 3 dc in next 5-ch sp, 1 ch, [1 dc, 2 ch, 1 dc] in next 5-ch sp, * rep from * to * 4 more times, 1 ch, 3 dc in next 5-ch sp, 1 ch, ss in 3rd of 5 ch.

**Round 4:** Ss into 2-ch sp, 5 ch, 1 dc in same ch sp, * 1 ch, 1 dc in next dc, 3 dc in next dc, 1 dc in next dc, 1 ch, # [1 dc, 2 ch, 1 dc] in next 2-ch sp, * rep from * to * 4 more times, then once again from * to #, ss in 3rd of 5 ch.

**Round 5:** Ss into 2-ch sp, 5 ch, 1 dc in same ch sp, * 1 ch, 1 dc in each of 2 dc, 3 dc in next dc, 1 dc in each of 2 dc, 1 ch, # [1 dc, 2 ch, 1 dc] in next 2-ch sp, * rep from * to * 4 more times, then once again from * to #, ss in 3rd of 5 ch.

**Round 6:** Ss into 2-ch sp, 5 ch, 1 dc in same ch sp, * 3 ch, 1 dc in each of 2 dc, 2 dc tog over [next and alt dc], 1 dc in each of 2 dc, 3 ch, # [1 dc, 2 ch, 1 dc] in next 2-ch sp, * rep from * to * 4 more times, then once again from * to #, ss in 3rd of 5 ch.

**Round 7:** Ss into 2-ch sp, 4 ch, 1 sc in same ch sp, * 4 ch, 1 sc in 3-ch sp, 4 ch, 3 dc tog over [first, 3rd, and 5th] of next 5 sts, 5 ch, ss in top of 3 dc tog, 4 ch, 1 sc in 3-ch sp, 4 ch, # [1 sc, 3 ch, 1 sc] in 2-ch sp, * rep from * to * 4 more times, then once again from * to #, ss in first of 4 ch.
Fasten off.

Blocks can be joined using the joining with picots method (see page 21).

# 60 BOBBLE FLOWER HEXAGON
*directory view page 37*

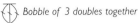

A B C

**Skill level:** intermediate
**Method of working:** in the round

**Key:**
Ω Fingerwrap
⌒ Chain
• Slip stitch
+ Single
† Double

⬦ Bobble of 3 doubles together
↶ Turn over
▷ Start/join in new color
◀ Fasten off

## METHOD

**Special abbreviation**
**B (bobble):** 3 dc tog in same place.

Using A, make a fingerwrap.
**Round 1:** 4 ch, [1 tr into wrap, 1 ch] 11 times, ss in 3rd of 4 ch. 24 sts. Fasten off A. Join yarn B to any tr.
**Round 2:** 3 ch, * [1 sc in next 1-ch sp, 1 sc in next tr] twice, 2 ch, * rep from * to * 4 more times, 1 sc in next 1-ch sp, 1 sc in next tr, 1 sc in next 1-ch sp, ss in first of 3 ch. 36 sts.
**Round 3:** 3 ch, * 1 sc in 2-ch sp, [B in next sc, 1 sc in next sc] twice, 2 ch, * rep from * to * 4 more times, 1 sc in 2-ch sp, B in next sc, 1 sc in next sc, B in next sc, ss in first of 3 ch. 42 sts.
**Round 4:** 3 ch, * 1 sc in 2-ch sp, [1 sc in next sc, 1 sc in B] twice, # 1 sc in next sc, 2 ch, * rep from * to * 4 more times, then once again from * to #, ss in first of 3 ch. 48 sts.
**Round 5:** 3 ch, * 1 sc in 2-ch sp, [B in next sc, 1 sc in next sc] 3 times, 2 ch, * rep from * to * 4 more times, 1 sc in 2-ch sp, [B in next sc, 1 sc in next sc] twice, B in next sc, ss in first of 3 ch. 54 sts.
Fasten off yarn B.

Turn flower over and join C to any 2-ch sp. Right side is now facing.
**Round 6:** 3 ch, * [1 sc in next sc, 1 sc in B] 3 times, 1 sc in next sc, # 1 sc in 2-ch sp, 2 ch, * rep from * to * 4 more times, then once again from * to #, ss in first of 3 ch. 60 sts.
**Round 7:** Ss into 2-ch sp, 5 ch, * [1 dc in next sc, 1 ch, sk 1 sc] 4 times, 1 dc in 2-ch sp, 2 ch, * rep from * to * 4 more times, [1 dc in next sc, 1 ch, sk 1 sc] 4 times, ss in 3rd of 5 ch. 66 sts.
**Round 8:** Ss into 2-ch sp, 5 ch, * [1 dc in next dc, 1 ch, sk 1 ch] 5 times, 1 dc in 2-ch sp, 2 ch, * rep from * to * 4 more times, [1 dc in next dc, 1 ch, sk 1 ch] 5 times, ss in 3rd of 5 ch. 78 sts.
**Round 9:** Ss into 2-ch sp, 5 ch, * [1 dc in next dc, 1 ch, sk 1 ch] 6 times, 1 dc in 2-ch sp, 2 ch, * rep from * to * 4 more times, [1 dc in next dc, 1 ch, sk 1 ch] 6 times, ss in 3rd of 5 ch. 90 sts.
Fasten off C.

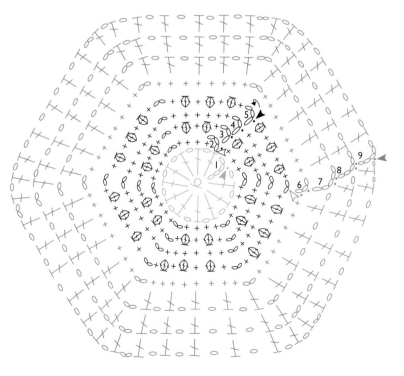

## 61 OPEN FLOWER HEXAGON

*directory view page 48*

**Skill level:** easy
**Method of working:** in the round

**Key:**

⌒ *Chain*

• *Slip stitch*

+ *Single*

† *Double*

‡ *Double treble*

◄ *Fasten off*

## METHOD

Make 6 ch, join into a ring with ss in first ch.
**Round 1:** 1 ch, 11 sc into ring. 12 sts.
**Round 2:** 1 ch, [7 ch, sk 1 sc, 1 sc in next sc] 5 times, 2 ch, 1 dtr in first ch of round. 6 petals.
**Round 3:** 3 ch, 4 dc under dtr, [3 ch, 5 dc in 7-ch sp] 5 times, 3 ch, ss in 3rd of 3 ch.
**Round 4:** 3 ch, 1 dc in each of 4 dc, [3 ch, 1 sc in 3-ch sp, 3 ch, 1 dc in each of 5 dc] 5 times, 3 ch, 1 sc in 3-ch sp, 3 ch, ss in 3rd of 3 ch.
**Round 5:** 2 ch, 4 dc tog over next

4 dc, * [5 ch, 1 sc in next 3-ch sp] twice, # 5 ch, 5 dc tog over next 5 dc, * rep from * to * 4 more times, then once again from * to #, 2 ch, 1 dc in 4 dc tog.
**Round 6:** 1 ch, [5 ch, 1 sc in next ch sp] 17 times, 2 ch, 1 dc in first ch. 18 ch sps.
**Round 7:** 1 ch, * 1 ch, [4 sc, 3 ch, 4 sc] in next 5-ch sp, 1 ch, 1 sc in next 5-ch sp, 5 ch, # 1 sc in next 5-ch sp, * rep from * to * 4 more times, then once again from * to #, ss in first ch.
Fasten off.

### MIX AND MATCH: 61 + 54

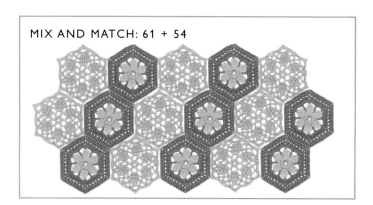

# 62 SPINNING DAHLIA HEXAGON

*directory view page 49*

A B

**Skill level:** intermediate
**Method of working:** in rows and in the round

**Key:**

| | | | |
|---|---|---|---|
| ⌒ | Chain | | Treble |
| • | Slip stitch | | Treble in back loop |
| + | Single | | Double treble |
| ⊼ | Single in back loop | | Double treble in back loop |
| | Half double | ▷ | Start/join in new color |
| | Half double in back loop | ◀ | Fasten off |
| | Double | ↵ | Direction of working |
| | Double in back loop | | |

## METHOD

Using A, make 17 ch, join into a ring with ss in 10<sup>th</sup> ch from hook, then continue along rem 7 ch:

**Row 1:** 1 sc in next st, 1 hdc in next st, 1 dc in next st, 2 dc in next st, 1 tr in next st, 2 tr in next st, 2 dtr in next st, turn. 10 sts.

**Row 2:** 2 ch, 1 sc in space between first and 2<sup>nd</sup> sts, [1 sc in next sp between 2 sts] 8 times, ss in sc at beg of row 1, ss into ring, turn. First petal made.

**Row 3:** Sk 1 ss, beg in back loop of next ss work as row 1 into back loops of 7 sts.

**Row 4:** As row 2. 2<sup>nd</sup> petal made. Rep rows 3–4 ten more times. 12 petals made.

Fasten off leaving a long tail. Run the tail through the ss worked into the ring and pull up firmly, then slip stitch the chain edge behind the top of the last row.

Join B to the tip of any petal.

**Round 1:** 1 ch, * [1 dtr, 4 ch, 1 dtr] in base of dtr at end of same petal, 1 sc in tip of next petal, * rep from * to ending ss in first ch.

**Round 2:** 5 ch, 1 dc in same place, * 4 ch, 1 sc in next 4-ch sp, 1 sc in dtr, 1 sc in sc, 1 sc in dtr, 1 sc in next 4-ch sp, 4 ch, [1 dc, 2 ch, 1 dc] in next sc, * rep from * to * 4 more times, 4 ch, 1 sc in next 4-ch sp, 1 sc in dtr, 1 sc in sc, 1 sc in dtr, 1 sc in next 4-ch sp, 4 ch, ss in 3<sup>rd</sup> of 5 ch. Fasten off B.

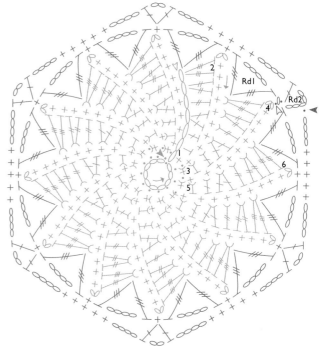

## 63 SWIRLING HEXAGON
*directory view page 34*

**Skill level:** intermediate
**Method of working:**
in the round

**Key:**
⌒ *Chain*
• *Slip stitch*
+ *Single*
⊤ *Double*

▷ *Start/join in new color*
◄ *Fasten off*
↩ *Direction of working*

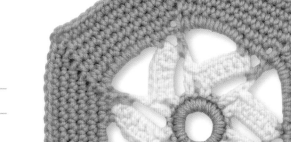

## METHOD

Using A, make 12 ch, join into a ring with ss in first ch.
**Round 1:** 1 ch, 23 sc into ring, ss in first ch. 24 sts.
Fasten off A. Join B to any sc.
**Round 2:** 9 ch, * sk first sc, 1 sc in next sc, turn, 1 ch, 5 sc in ch sp, turn, 1 ch, sk 1 sc, 1 sc in each of 4 sc, 1 sc in 1 ch (a petal made), sk 1 sc of round 1, # 1 dc in next sc, 6 ch, * rep from * to * 4 more times, then once again from * to #, ss in 3$^{rd}$ of 9 ch. 6 petals.
Fasten off B. Join C to 6-ch sp at end of any petal.
**Round 3:** 5 ch, [1 sc in 1 ch at tip of same petal, 7 ch, 1 dc in 6-ch sp at end of next petal, 2 ch] 5 times, 1 sc in 1 ch at tip of same petal, 7 ch, ss in 3$^{rd}$ of 5 ch.
**Round 4:** 3 ch, * 1 sc in 2-ch sp, 1 sc in next sc, 7 sc in 7-ch sp, # 1 sc in dc, 2 ch, * rep from * to * 4 more times, then once again from * to #, ss in first of 3 ch. 10 sc on each side.

**Round 5:** 3 ch, * 1 sc in 2-ch sp, 1 sc in each sc to next 2-ch sp, 2 ch, * rep from * to * 4 more times, 1 sc in 2-ch sp, 1 sc in each sc, ss in first of 3 ch. 11 sc on each side.
Rep round 5 four more times.
15 sc on each side.
Fasten off C.

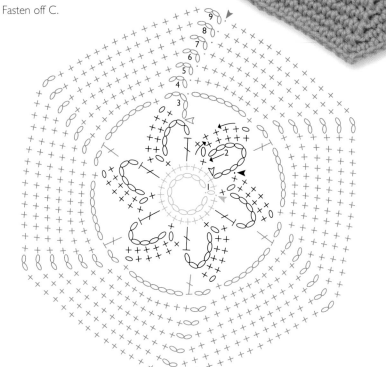

# 64 SPRING MEADOW HEXAGON
*directory view page 33*

**A B C**

**Skill level:** easy
**Method of working:** in the round

**Key:**
- ⌒ Chain
- • Slip stitch
- ⊤ Double
- Starting popcorn
- Popcorn of 4 doubles
- ▷ Start/join in new color
- ◀ Fasten off

## METHOD

**Special abbreviations**

**PC (4-dc popcorn):** 4 dc in same place (as given), remove hook from working loop and insert it through top of first of these sts, catch working loop and pull it through tightly.

**SPC (starting popcorn):** 3 ch, 3 dc in same place (as given), remove hook from working loop and insert through 3rd of 3 ch, catch working loop and pull it through tightly.

Using A, make 6 ch, join into a ring with ss in first ch.
**Round 1:** SPC into ring, [3 ch, PC into ring] 5 times, 3 ch, ss into top of SPC.
Fasten off A. Join B to any 3-ch sp.
**Round 2:** 5 ch, [5 dc in next ch sp, 2 ch] 5 times, 4 dc in next ch sp, ss in 3rd of 5 ch.
**Round 3:** Ss into 2-ch sp, 5 ch, 1 dc in same ch sp, * 1 dc in each of 2 dc, 1 ch, sk 1 dc, 1 dc in each of 2 dc, # [1 dc, 2 ch, 1 dc] in next 2-ch sp, * rep from * to * 4 more times, then once again from * to #, ss in 3rd of 5 ch.
Fasten off B. Join C to any 2-ch sp.

**Round 4:** [SPC, 3 ch, PC] into 2-ch sp, * 3 ch, PC into next 1-ch sp, 3 ch, # [PC, 3 ch, PC] into next 2-ch sp, * rep from * to * 4 more times, then once again from * to #, ss into top of SPC.
Fasten off C. Join B to any corner 3-ch sp between 2 PC in same place.
**Round 5:** 5 ch, 2 dc in same ch sp, * [1 ch, 3 dc in next 3-ch sp] twice, 1 ch, # [2 dc, 3 ch, 2 dc] in corner 3-ch sp, * rep from * to * 4 more times, then once again from * to #, 1 dc in next ch sp, ss in 3rd of 5 ch.
**Round 6:** Ss into 2-ch sp, 5 ch, 1 dc in same ch sp, * [1 dc, 1 ch, 1 dc] in each of three 1-ch sps, # [1 dc, 2 ch, 1 dc] in next 2-ch sp, * rep from * to * 4 more times, then once again from * to #, ss in 3rd of 5 ch.
**Round 7:** Ss into 2-ch sp, 5 ch, 1 dc in same ch sp, * [1 dc between next and foll dc, 3 dc in 1-ch sp] 3 times, 1 dc between next and foll dc, # [1 dc, 2 ch, 1 dc] in 2-ch sp, * rep from * to * 4 more times, then once again from * to #, ss in 3rd of 5 ch.
15 dc on each side.
Fasten off C.

# 65 OPEN DAHLIA HEXAGON

*directory view page 51*

A B C

**Skill level:** easy
**Method of working:** in the round

**Key:**

- *Chain*
- • *Slip stitch*
- + *Single*
- *2 singles together*
- *3 singles together*
- ▷ *Start/join in new color*
- ◀ *Fasten off*

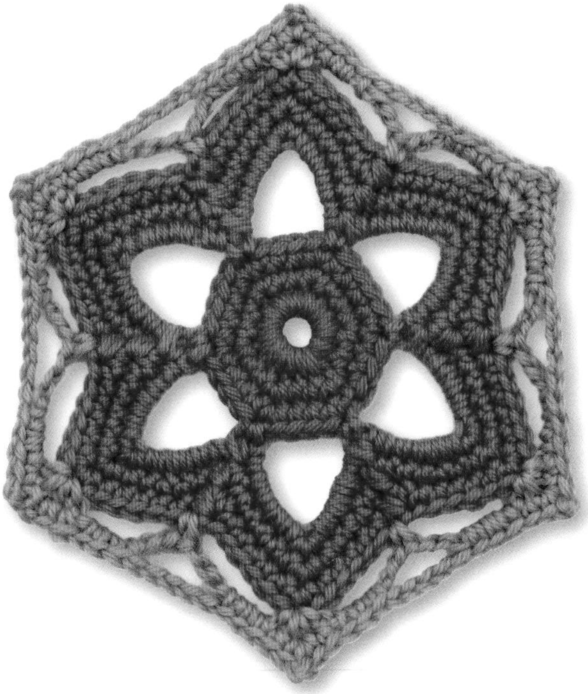

## METHOD

Using A, make 6 ch, join into a ring with ss in first ch.

**Round 1:** 1 ch, 17 sc into ring, ss in first ch. 18 sts.

**Round 2:** 1 ch, 1 sc in same place, [1 sc in each of 2 sc, 2 sc in next sc] 5 times, 1 sc in each of 2 sc, ss in first ch. 24 sts.

**Round 3:** 1 ch, 1 sc in same place, [1 sc in each of 3 sc, 2 sc in next sc] 5 times, 1 sc in each of 3 sc, ss in first ch. 30 sts.

Fasten off A. Join B to any sc that is the first of 2 sc in same place.

**Round 4:** 10 ch, [sk 4 sc, 1 sc in next sc, 9 ch] 5 times, sk 4 sc, ss in first of 10 ch. 6 ch loops.

**Round 5:** Ss into 9-ch sp, 1 ch, * 5 sc in 9-ch loop, 3 sc in 5th of these 9 ch, 5 sc in same ch loop, # 3 sc tog over [same ch loop, next sc, and foll ch loop], * rep from * to * 4 more times, then once again from * to #, 2 sc tog over same ch loop and next sc, ss in first ch. 84 sts.

**Round 6:** 1 ch, sk first sc, * 1 sc in each of 5 sc, 3 sc in next sc (center sc of 3 in same place), 1 sc in each of 5 sc, # 3 sc tog over next 3 sc, * rep from * to * 4 more times, then once again from * to #, 2 sc tog over last 2 sts, ss in first ch. 84 sts.

**Round 7:** As round 6. 6 petals. Fasten off B. Join C to center sc of 3 in same place at tip of any petal.

**Round 8:** 3 ch, 1 sc in same place, * 6 ch, sk 5 sc, 1 sc in 3 sc tog, 6 ch, sk 5 sc, # [1 sc, 2 ch, 1 sc] in next sc (center sc of 3 in same place), * rep from * to * 4 more times, then once again from * to #, ss in first of 3 ch. 12 ch loops.

**Round 9:** Ss into 2-ch sp, 3 ch, 1 sc in same place, * 1 sc in next sc, 3 sc in 5-ch loop, 5 ch, 3 sc in next 6-ch loop, # 1 sc in next sc, [1 sc, 2 ch, 1 sc] in 2-ch loop, * rep from * to * 4 more times, then once again from * to #, 1 sc in st closing previous round, ss in first of 3 ch. Fasten off C.

Blocks may be joined using the joining with picots method, page 21.

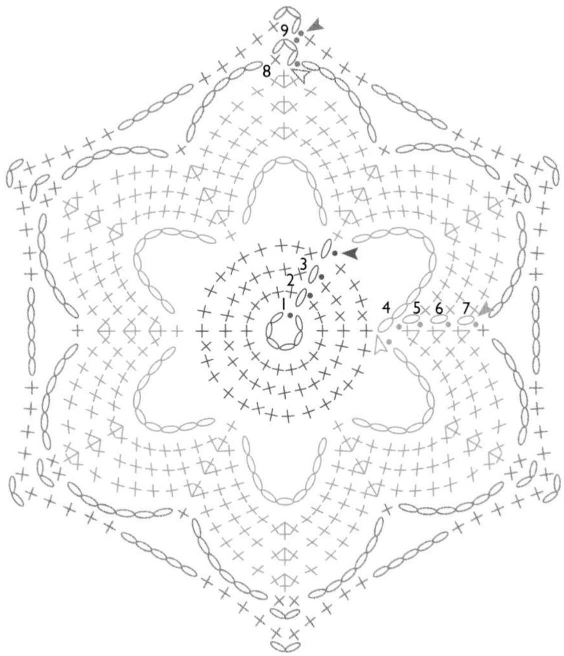

**HELENIUM CIRCLE**
*directory view page 48*

A B C

**Skill level:** easy
**Method of working:**
in the round

**Key:**
○ *Fingerwrap*
⌒ *Chain*
· *Slip stitch*
+ *Single*
⊺ *Double*

*Popcorn of 4 trebles*
▷ *Start/join in new color*
◀ *Fasten off*

## METHOD

**Special abbreviation**
**PC (4-tr popcorn):** 4 tr in same place (as given), remove hook from working loop and insert it through top of first of these sts, catch working loop and pull it through tightly.

Using A, make a fingerwrap.
**Round 1:** 3 ch, 15 dc into wrap, ss in 3$^{rd}$ of 3 ch. 16 sts.
**Round 2:** 4 ch, [1 dc, 1 ch] in each of 15 dc, ss in 3$^{rd}$ of 4 ch. Fasten off A. Join B to any 1-ch sp.
**Round 3:** 4 ch, 3 tr in same sp, remove hook from working loop and insert through 4$^{th}$ of 4 ch, catch working loop and pull it through, [3 ch, PC in next ch sp] 15 times, 3 ch, ss in 4$^{th}$ of 4 ch at beg of round.

Fasten off B. Join C to any 3-ch sp.
**Round 4:** 1 ch, 3 sc in same ch sp, [5 ch, 4 sc in next ch sp] 15 times, 2 ch, 1 dc in first ch of round.
**Round 5:** 1 ch, [4 ch, 1 sc in next 5-ch loop] 15 times, 4 ch, ss in first ch of round.
**Round 6:** Ss into next 4-ch sp, 1 ch, 4 sc in same ch sp, [5 ch, 5 sc in next ch sp] 15 times, 5 ch, ss in first ch of round.
Fasten off C.

## 67 ROSETTE CIRCLE

*directory view page 36*

**Skill level:** easy
**Method of working:** in the round

**Key:**
- *Chain*
- *Slip stitch*
- *Single*
- *Single under both chain loops below*
- *Half double*
- *Double*
- *2 doubles together in same place*
- *Treble*
- *Fasten off*

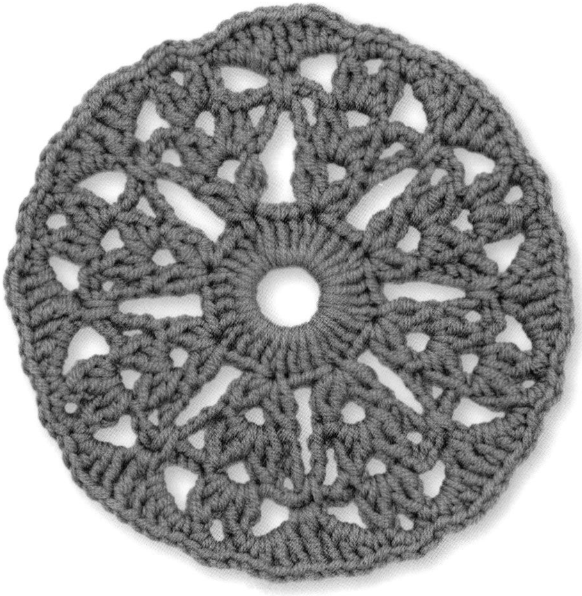

### METHOD

Make 12 ch, join into a ring with ss in first ch.

**Round 1:** 3 ch, 31 dc into ring, ss in 3rd of 3 ch. 32 sts.

**Round 2:** 2 ch, [1 dc, 3 ch, 2 dc tog] in same place as base of 2 ch, * 7 ch, sk 3 dc, [2 dc tog, 3 ch, 2 dc tog] in next dc, * rep from * to * 6 more times, 7 ch, sk 3 dc, ss in first dc of round. 8 sections.

**Round 3:** Ss into 3-ch sp, 2 ch, [1 dc, 3 ch, 2 dc tog] in same ch sp, * 7 ch, [2 dc tog, 3 ch, 2 dc tog] in next 3-ch sp, * rep from * to * 6 more times, 7 ch, ss in first dc.

**Round 4:** Ss into 3-ch sp, 2 ch, [1 dc, 3 ch, 2 dc tog] in same ch sp, * 4 ch, 1 sc under both 7-ch loops, 4 ch, # [2 dc tog, 3 ch, 2 dc tog] in next 3-ch sp, * rep from * to * 6 more times, then once again from * to #, ss in first dc.

**Round 5:** Ss into 3-ch sp, 1 ch, 2 sc in same ch sp, * [1 sc, 1 hdc, 2 dc] in 4-ch sp, 1 tr in sc, [2 dc, 1 hdc, 1 sc] in 4-ch sp, # 3 sc in 3-ch sp, * rep from * to * 6 more times, then once again from * to #, ss in first ch. 96 sts.

Fasten off.

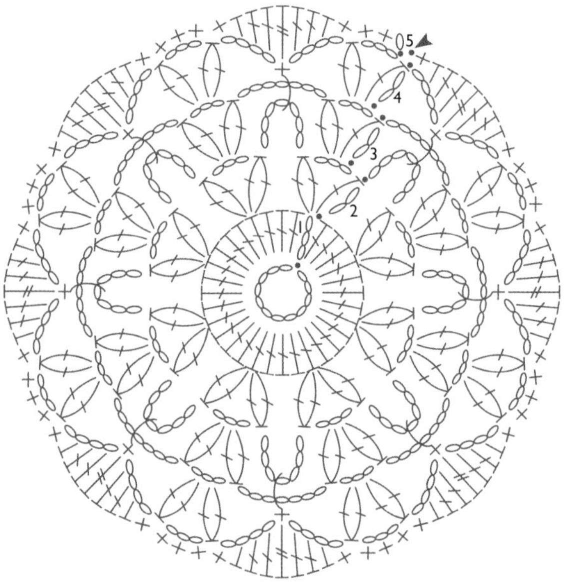


### MIX AND MATCH: 67 + 78

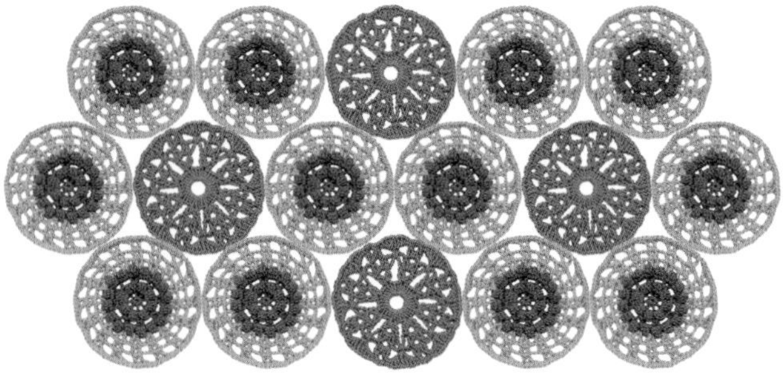

# (68) CELTIC FLOWER CIRCLE
*directory view page 49*

A  B  C

**Skill level:** easy
**Method of working:**
in the round

**Key:**
⌢ *Chain*
• *Slip stitch*
+ *Single*
† *Double*
‡ *Treble*

▷ *Start/join in new color*
◀ *Fasten off*

## METHOD

Using A, make 6 ch, join into a ring with ss in first ch.
**Round 1:** 1 ch, [3 ch, 2 tr into ring, 3 ch, 1 sc into ring] 3 times, 3 ch, 2 tr into ring, 3 ch, ss in first ch of round. 4 petals.
Fasten off A. Join B to sc between any 2 petals.
**Round 2:** 6 ch, 1 dc in same place, [3 ch, sk 1 petal, [1 dc, 3 ch, 1 dc] in next sc] 3 times, 3 ch, sk 1 petal, ss in 3rd of 6 ch. 8 loops.
**Round 3:** 4 ch, [3 dc in next 3-ch sp, 3 ch, 1 sc in next dc, 3 ch] 7 times, 3 dc in next 3-ch sp, 3 ch, ss in first of 4 ch. 8 petals.
Fasten off B. Join C to any sc before 3 dc worked into a ch sp over a petal.

**Round 4:** Work behind round 3: 1 ch, [4 ch, sk 1 petal, 1 sc in next sc] 7 times, 4 ch, ss in first ch.
**Round 5:** 6 ch, [6 tr in next 4-ch sp, 2 ch,] 7 times, 5 tr in last 4-ch sp, ss in 4th of 6 ch.
**Round 6:** Ss into 2-ch sp, 8 ch, ss in 4th ch from hook, 1 tr in same ch sp, * 1 tr in each of 6 tr, [1 tr, 4 ch, ss in 4th ch from hook, 1 tr] in next 2-ch sp, * rep from * to * 6 more times, 1 tr in each of 6 tr, ss in 4th of 8 ch.
Fasten off C.

Blocks may be joined using the joining with picots method, page 21.

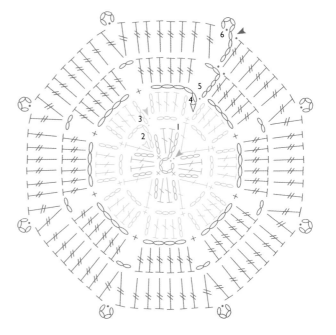

## 69 THISTLE CIRCLE
*directory view page 47*

A  B  C

**Skill level:** intermediate
**Method of working:** in the round

**Key:**
- ○ *Fingerwrap*
- ⌢ *Chain*
- • *Slip stitch*
- + *Single*
- ⦶ *Puff stitch of 4 half doubles together*
- ⊤ *Double*
- ⋀ *2 doubles together*
- ⋔ *2 doubles together in same place*
- ⊤ *Treble*
- ⨎ *Front-raised treble*
- ▷ *Start/join in new color*
- ◀ *Fasten off*

## METHOD

**Special abbreviation**
**PS (puff stitch):** 4 hdc tog in same place.
**frtr (front raised tr):** inserting hook from front, work 1 tr around post of given st.

Using A, make a fingerwrap.
**Round 1:** 4 ch, [1 dc into wrap, 1 ch] 15 times, ss in 3rd of 4 ch. 32 sts.
**Round 2:** 5 ch, [1 frtr in next dc, 2 ch, 1 dc in next dc, 2 ch] 7 times, 1 frtr in next dc, 2 ch, ss in 3rd of 5 ch. 48 sts.
**Round 3:** 3 ch, * [2 dc tog, 2 ch, 1 frtr; 2 ch, 2 dc tog] all in next frtr; # 1 dc in next dc, * rep from * to * 6 more times, then once again from * to #, ss in 3rd of 3 ch.
**Round 4:** Ss into sp before next 2 dc tog, 7 ch, * sk [2 dc tog, 2 ch], PS in next frtr; 5 ch, # 2 dc tog, inserting hook between next 2 dc tog and 1 dc, then between same dc and foll 2 dc tog; 4 ch, * rep from * to * 6 more times, then once again from * to #, 1 dc between 2 dc tog and 7 ch, ss in 3rd of 7 ch.

Fasten off A. Join B to any 2 dc tog.
**Round 5:** 2 ch, * 7 tr in next PS, 1 ch, # 1 sc in next 2 dc tog, 1 ch, * rep from * to * 6 more times, then once again from * to #, ss in first ch. 80 sts.
Fasten off B. Join C to 1-ch sp to right of any sc.
**Round 6:** 2 ch, sk 1 sc, 1 dc in next 1-ch sp, * 5 ch, 1 sc in center tr of 7, 5 ch, # 2 dc tog over [next 1-ch sp and foll 1-ch sp], * rep from * to * 6 more times, then once again from * to #, ss in first dc. 96 sts.
**Round 7:** 1 ch, * 5 sc in 5-ch sp, 1 sc in next sc, 5 sc in 5-ch sp, # 1 sc in 2 dc tog, * rep from * to * 6 more times, then once again from * to #, ss in first ch. 96 sts.
Fasten off C.

# 70 DAHLIA CIRCLE

*directory view page 50*

**Skill level:** easy

**Method of working:** in the round

**Key:**

- ⌒ Chain
- • Slip stitch
- + Single
- ⊤ Half double
- ⊥ Double
- ⋏ 3 doubles together
- Treble
- ◄ Fasten off

## METHOD

**Special abbreviation**
**3-ch P (3-ch picot):** 3 ch, ss in st at base of these 3 ch.

Make 8 ch, join into a ring with ss in first ch.

**Round 1:** 3 ch, 23 dc into ring, ss in 3rd of 3 ch. 24 sts.

**Round 2:** 3 ch, sk 1 dc, [1 sc in next dc, 2 ch, sk 1 dc] 11 times, ss in first of 3 ch. 12 ch sps.

**Round 3:** Ss into 2-ch sp, 2 ch, 2 dc tog in same 2-ch sp, [4 ch, 3 dc tog in next 2-ch sp] 11 times, 2 ch, 1 hdc in top of 2 dc tog. 12 petals.

**Round 4:** 1 ch, [5 ch, 1 sc in next 4-ch sp] 11 times, 2 ch, 1 dc in first ch. 12 ch sps.

**Round 5:** 1 ch, [6 ch, 1 sc in next 5-ch sp] 11 times, 3 ch, 1 dc in first ch.

**Round 6:** 1 ch, [7 ch, 1 sc in next 6-ch sp] 11 times, 3 ch, 1 tr in first ch.

**Round 7:** 4 ch, ss in first of these 4 ch, [8 ch, 1 sc in next 7-ch sp, 3-ch P] 11 times, 8 ch, ss in first ch. Fasten off.

## 71 FLORAL CIRCLE
*directory view page 45*

A B C

**Skill level:** easy
**Method of working:** in the round

**Key:**
- ○ *Chain*
- • *Slip stitch*
- + *Single*
- ⊤ *Half double*
- ⊤ *Double*
- ⬙ *2 doubles together*
- ⊤ *Treble*
- ▷ *Start/join in new color*
- ◄ *Fasten off*

## METHOD

Using A, make 8 ch, join into a ring with ss in first ch.

**Round 1:** 1 ch, 15 sc into ring, ss in first ch. 16 sts.

**Round 2:** 2 ch, 1 dc in same place as base of 2 ch, [5 ch, sk 1 sc, 2 dc tog in next sc] 7 times, 5 ch, sk last sc, ss in first dc. 8 ch sps. Fasten off A. Join B to any 5-ch sp.

**Round 3:** 1 ch, [1 hdc, 1 dc, 2 tr, 1 ch, 2 tr, 1 dc, 1 hdc, 1 sc] in same ch sp, [1 sc, 1 hdc, 1 dc, 2 tr, 1 ch, 2 tr, 1 dc, 1 hdc, 1 sc] in each of 7 rem ch sps, ss in first ch. 8 petals. Fasten off B. Join C to 1-ch sp at tip of any petal.

**Round 4:** 5 ch, [1 tr between next 2 sc where petals join, 4 ch, 1 sc in next 1-ch sp, 4 ch] 7 times, 1 tr between 2 sc, 4 ch, ss in first of 5 ch.

**Round 5:** 5 ch, 1 dc in same place as base of these 5 ch, * 2 ch, [1 dc, 2 ch, 1 dc] in next tr, 2 ch, # [1 dc, 2 ch, 1 dc] in next sc, * rep from * to * 6 more times, then once again from * to #, ss in first of 5 ch.

**Round 6:** Ss into 2-ch sp, 3 ch, 2 dc in same ch sp, 3 dc in each 2-ch sp, ss in 3rd of 3 ch. 96 sts. Fasten off C.

**Skill level:** intermediate
**Method of working:** in the round

**Key:**
Ω  Fingerwrap
◯  Chain
•  Slip stitch
+  Single
†  Double
‡  Treble

▯  Bullion stitch
▥  Popcorn of 5 trebles
▷  Start/join in new color
◀  Fasten off

## METHOD

**Special abbreviations**
**BS (bullion stitch):** yrh 5 times, insert hook as directed, yrh, pull through all 6 loops on hook.
**PC (5-tr popcorn):** 5 tr in same place (as given), remove hook from working loop and insert it through top of first of these sts, catch working loop and pull it through tightly.

Using A, make a fingerwrap.
**Round 1:** 4 ch, 15 tr into wrap, ss in 4th of 4 ch. 16 sts.
Fasten off A. Join B to any tr.
**Round 2:** 4 ch, [BS in next tr, 1 ch] 15 times, BS in same place as base of 4 ch, ss in 3$^{rd}$ of 4 ch. 32 sts.
Fasten off B. Join C to any 1-ch sp.
**Round 3:** 3 ch, [sk BS, 1 sc in next 1-ch sp, 2 ch] 15 times, ss in first of 3 ch. 48 sts.
**Round 4:** Ss into 2-ch sp, 4 ch, 4 tr in same ch sp, remove hook from working loop and insert through 4$^{th}$ of 4 ch, catch working loop and pull it through (starting PC made), [4 ch, sk 1 sc, PC in next 2-ch sp] 15 times, 4 ch, ss in top of starting PC. 16 PC, 80 sts.
Fasten off C. Join D to any 4-ch sp.

**Round 5:** 1 ch, 4 sc in same ch sp, [1 ch, sk PC, 5 sc in next ch sp] 15 times, 1 ch, sk PC, ss in first ch. 96 sts.
**Round 6:** 4 ch, sk 1 sc, * BS in next sc, 1 ch, sk 1 sc, 1 dc in next sc, 1 dc in 1-ch sp, # 1 dc in next sc, 1 ch, sk 1 sc, * rep from * to * 14 more times, then once again from * to #, ss in 3$^{rd}$ of 4 ch.
**Round 7:** 1 ch, 1 sc in each st and 1-ch sp all around, ending ss in first ch. 96 sts.
Fasten off D.

## 73 BUTTERFLY CIRCLE
*directory view page 45*

A B C

**Skill level:** intermediate
**Method of working:** in the round

**Key:**

◠ *Chain*

• *Slip stitch*

+ *Single*

⌓ *Single through center of stitch below*

┬ *Half double*

╪ *Double*

⋔ *3 trebles together*

⋔ *2 double trebles together*

╪ *Triple treble*

▷ *Start/join in new color*

◄ *Fasten off*

## METHOD

Using A, make 6 ch, join into a ring with ss in first ch.
**Round 1:** 3 ch, 15 dc into ring, ss in 3$^{rd}$ of 3 ch. 16 dc.
**Round 2:** 6 ch, sk 1 dc, 1 sc in next dc, [5 ch, sk 1 dc, 1 sc in next dc] 6 times, 2 ch, sk 1 dc, 1 dc in first of 6 ch. 8 loops.
**Round 3:** 4 ch, * [1 sc, 5 ch, 1 sc] in next 5-ch sp, 3 ch, * rep from * to * 6 more times, 1 sc, 5 ch, ss in first of 4 ch.
Fasten off A. Join B to any 5-ch loop.
**Round 4:** 3 ch, 2 tr tog in same ch loop, * sk 3-ch loop, [3 tr tog, 11 ch, 3 tr tog] in next 5-ch loop, * rep from * to * 6 more times, 3 tr tog in first ch loop, 5 ch, 1 ttr in 2 tr tog at beg of round. 16 groups = 8 pairs of wings.

**Round 5:** * [2 dtr tog, 3 ch, 1 loose hdc, 3 ch, 2 dtr tog] in st closing next group, ss in 6$^{th}$ of 11 ch, * rep from * to * 7 more times, working final ss in top of ttr.
Fasten off B. Join C to any 3-ch sp before a loose hdc.
**Round 6:** 1 ch, 3 sc in same ch sp, * 1 sc down through center of loose hdc, 4 sc in next 3-ch sp, 1 ch, 1 sc between next 2 groups, 3 ch, ss in last sc, 1 ch, 4 sc in next 3-ch sp, * rep from * to * 6 more times, 1 ch, 1 sc between 2 groups, 3 ch, ss in last sc, 1 ch, ss in first ch of round. 96 sts.
Fasten off C.

Blocks can be joined using the joining with picots method (see page 21).

# 74 POPCORN FLOWER CIRCLE
*directory view page 40*

**Skill level:** easy
**Method of working:** in the round

**Key:**

⬯ *Chain*

• *Slip stitch*

+ *Single*

⊤ *Double*

 *Popcorn of 4 doubles*

◀ *Fasten off*

## METHOD

**Special abbreviation**
**PC (4-dc popcorn):** 4 dc in same place (as given), remove hook from working loop and insert it through top of first of these sts, catch working loop and pull it through tightly.

Make 4 ch, join into a ring with ss in first ch.
**Round 1:** 3 ch, 15 dc into ring, ss in 3rd of 3 ch.
**Round 2:** 6 ch, 1 dc in st at base of these ch, 1 ch, * PC in next dc, 1 ch, [1 dc, 3 ch, 1 dc] in next dc, 1 ch, * rep from * to * 6 more times, PC in last dc, 1 ch, ss in 3rd of 6 ch.
**Round 3:** Ss into next ch sp, 8 ch, 1 dc in same ch sp, * 1 ch, PC in next dc, 1 ch, sk 1 PC, PC in next dc, 1 ch, # [1 dc, 5 ch, 1 dc] in next 3-ch sp, * rep from * to * 6 more times, then once again from * to #, ss in 3rd of 8 ch.

**Round 4:** Ss into next ch sp, 10 ch, 1 dc in same ch sp, * 1 ch, PC in next dc, 1 ch, sk 2 PC, PC in next dc, 1 ch, # [1 dc, 7 ch, 1 dc] in next 5-ch sp, * rep from * to * 6 more times, then once again from * to #, ss in 3rd of 10 ch.
**Round 5:** Ss in each of next 4 ch, 6 ch, * PC in 1-ch sp between next 2 PC, 5 ch, 1 sc in next 7-ch sp, 5 ch, * rep from * to * 7 more times, ss in first of 6 ch.
**Round 6:** Ss into next ch sp, 1 ch, 5 sc in same ch sp, 6 sc in each ch sp, ending ss in first ch of round. 96 sts.
Fasten off.

## 75 BUTTERCUP CIRCLE
*directory view page 35*

A  B

**Skill level:** easy
**Method of working:**
in the round

**Key:**

$\Omega$   *Fingerwrap*

$\sim$   *Chain*

•   *Slip stitch*

+   *Single*

$\dagger$   *Double*

    *Double in*
    *stitch below*

  *Bobble of 3 trebles
together*

  *Turn over*

▷   *Start/join in new color*

◀   *Fasten off*

## METHOD

**Special abbreviation**
**B (bobble):** 3 tr tog in same place.

Using A, make a fingerwrap.
**Round 1:** 3 ch, 15 dc into wrap, ss in 3$^{rd}$ of 3 ch. 16 sts.
**Round 2:** 1 ch, [B in next dc, 1 sc in next dc] 7 times, B in next dc, ss in first ch. 8 bobbles.
Fasten off A. Turn flower over so bobbles are facing and join yarn B to dc of round 1 at base of any sc.
**Round 3:** 6 ch, [sk B, 1 dc in dc at base of next sc, 3 ch] 7 times, sk B, ss in 3$^{rd}$ of 6 ch. Eight 3-ch sps.
**Round 4:** 4 ch, [5 dc in next 3-ch sp, 1 ch, sk 1 dc] 7 times, 4 dc in last ch sp, ss in 3$^{rd}$ of 4 ch. 40 dc.

**Round 5:** Ss into 1-ch sp, 4 ch, 1 dc in same sp, * 1 dc in each of 5 dc, [1 dc, 1 ch, 1 dc] in 1-ch sp, * rep from * to * 6 more times, 1 dc in each of 5 dc, ss in 3$^{rd}$ of 4 ch. 56 dc.
**Round 6:** Ss into 1-ch sp, 4 ch, 1 dc in same sp, * 1 dc in each of 7 dc, [1 dc, 1 ch, 1 dc] in 1-ch sp, * rep from * to * 6 more times, 1 dc in each of 7 dc, ss in 3$^{rd}$ of 4 ch. 72 dc.
**Round 7:** Ss into 1-ch sp, 4 ch, 1 dc in same sp, * 1 dc in each of 9 dc, [1 dc, 1 ch, 1 dc] in 1-ch sp, * rep from * to * 6 more times, 1 dc in each of 9 dc, ss in 3$^{rd}$ of 4 ch. 88 dc, 96 sts.
Fasten off yarn B.

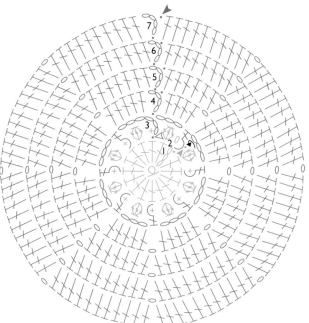

## 76 DANDELION CIRCLE

*directory view page 37*

A B

**Skill level:** intermediate
**Method of working:** in the round

Key:
- *Fingerwrap*
- *Chain*
- *Slip stitch*
- *Slip stitch in space below*
- *Single*
- *Treble*
- *5 trebles together*
- *[1 double, 1 treble, 1 double treble, 1 treble, 1 double] all worked together*
- *Start/join in new color*
- *Fasten off*

### METHOD

Using A, make a fingerwrap.
**Round 1:** 5 ch, [1 tr into wrap, 1 ch] 14 times, ss in 3rd of 4 ch. 30 sts.
Fasten off A. Join B to any tr.
**Round 2:** 1 ch, 1 sc in each ch sp and tr all around, ss in first ch. 30 sts.
**Round 3:** 1 ch, 1 sc in each of 2 sc, [9 ch, sk 2 sc, 1 sc in each of 3 sc] 5 times, 9 ch, sk 2 sc, ss in first ch. Six 9-ch loops.
Fasten off B. Join A to center sc of any 3 sc.
**Round 4:** 3 ch, 2 tr tog over first and 3rd ch of 9-ch loop, * 9 ch, 5 tr tog over [7th and 9th ch of same 9-ch loop, center sc of 3 sc, first and 3rd ch of next 9-ch loop], * rep from * to * 4 more times, 9 ch, 2 tr tog over [7th and 9th ch of same 9-ch loop], ss in 2 tr tog.
**Round 5:** 4 ch, [1 tr, 1 ch] 5 times in ch closing first 2 tr tog of round 4, ss in 9-ch loop of round 3 (enclosing ch of round 4), * 1 ch, [1 tr, 1 ch] 6 times in ch closing next 5 tr tog, ss in 9-ch loop of round 3 (enclosing ch of round 4), * rep from * to * 4 more times, 1 ch, ss in 3rd of 4 ch. 6 flowers complete.
Fasten off A. Join B to center 1-ch sp at top of any flower.
**Round 6:** 2 ch, sk 1 tr, 1 sc in 1-ch sp, * 5 ch, work 5 sts tog: [1 dc in next 1-ch sp, 1 tr in foll 1-ch sp, 1 dtr in ss between flowers, 1 tr in next 1-ch sp, 1 dc in foll 1-ch sp], 5 ch, # [1 sc in next 1-ch sp, 1 ch, sk 1 tr] twice, 1 sc in next ch sp, * rep from * to * 4 more times, then once again from * to #, 1 sc in next 1-ch sp, 1 ch, sk 1 tr, ss in first of 2 ch. 96 sts.
**Round 7:** 1 ch, 1 sc in 1-ch sp, * 5 sc in 5-ch sp, 1 sc in 5 sts tog, 5 sc in 5-ch sp, # [1 sc in next sc, 1 sc in 1-ch sp] twice, 1 sc in next sc, * rep from * to * 4 more times, then once again from * to #, 1 sc in next sc, 1 sc in 1-ch sp, ss in first ch. 96 sc.
Fasten off B.

**77** **CORAL FLOWER CIRCLE**
directory view page 38

A B

**Skill level:** easy
**Method of working:**
in the round

**Key:**
Ω  *Fingerwrap*
◠  *Chain*
•  *Slip stitch*
†  *Double*
▷  *Start/join in new color*
◀  *Fasten off*

## METHOD

Using A, make a fingerwrap.
**Round 1:** 3 ch, 23 dc into wrap, ss in 3$^{rd}$ of 3 ch.
**Round 2:** 3 ch, 1 dc in each of 2 dc, 3 ch, [1 dc in each of 3 dc, 3 ch] 7 times, ss in 3$^{rd}$ of 3 ch.
**Round 3:** 2 ch, 2 dc tog over next 2 dc, [3 ch, 1 dc in 3-ch sp, 3 ch, 3 dc tog over next 3 dc] 7 times, 3 ch, 1 dc in 3-ch sp, 3 ch, ss in first 2 dc tog of round.
Fasten off A. Join B to any 3-ch sp before a single dc.

**Round 4:** 4 ch, [3 dc in next 3-ch sp, 1 ch] 15 times, 2 dc in same ch sp as beg of round, ss in 3$^{rd}$ of 4 ch.
**Round 5:** Ss into 1-ch sp, 4 ch, [4 dc in next 1-ch sp, 1 ch] 15 times, 3 dc in same ch sp as beg of round, ss in 3$^{rd}$ of 4 ch.
**Round 6:** Ss into 1-ch sp, 4 ch, [5 dc in next 1-ch sp, 1 ch] 15 times, 4 dc in same ch sp as beg of round, ss in 3$^{rd}$ of 4 ch. 96 sts.
Fasten off B.

**MIX AND MATCH: 77 + 74**

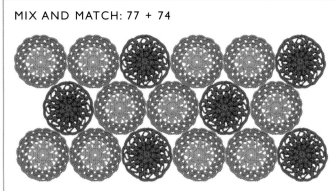

## 78 BOBBLE FLOWER CIRCLE
*directory view page 41*

A  B

**Skill level:** easy
**Method of working:**
in the round

**Key:**

⊂ *Chain*          ▷ *Start/join in new color*

• *Slip stitch*     ◄ *Fasten off*

+ *Single*          ↰ *Turn over work*

┬ *Double*

⬖ *Bobble of 4 doubles together*

## METHOD

**Special abbreviation**
**B (bobble):** 4 dc tog in same place.

Using A, make 4 ch, join into a ring with ss in first ch.
**Round 1:** 4 ch, [1 dc into ring, 1 ch] 7 times, ss in 3rd of 4 ch. 16 sts.
**Round 2:** 1 ch, [B in next 1-ch sp, 1 ch, 1 sc in next dc] 7 times, B in next 1-ch sp, 1 ch, ss in first ch. 8 bobbles.
**Round 3:** 4 ch, 1 dc in same place as base of these ch, * 1 ch, sk B and foll ch, [1 dc, 1 ch, 1 dc] in next sc, * rep from * to * 6 more times, 1 ch, sk B and foll ch, ss in 3rd of 4 ch.
**Round 4:** 1 ch, 1 sc in same place, [B in next 1-ch sp, 1 ch, 2 sc in next dc] 15 times, B in next 1-ch sp, ss in first ch. 16 bobbles.
Fasten off A. Turn work over and join yarn B to first of any 2 sc. Right side is now facing.

**Round 5:** 4 ch, 1 dc in same place as base of these ch, [1 ch, sk B and foll ch, 1 dc in next sc, 1 ch, 1 dc in next sc] 15 times, 1 ch, sk B and foll ch, ss in 3rd of 4 ch. 64 sts.
**Round 6:** Ss into 1-ch sp, 4 ch, 1 dc in same sp, * 2 ch, sk [1 dc, 1 ch, 1 dc], [1 dc, 1 ch, 1 dc] in next 1-ch sp, * rep from * to * 14 more times, 2 ch, sk [1 dc, 1 ch, 1 dc], ss in 3rd of 4 ch. 80 sts.
**Round 7:** Ss into 1-ch sp, 4 ch, 1 dc in same sp, * 3 ch, sk [1 dc, 2 ch, 1 dc], [1 dc, 1 ch, 1 dc] in 1-ch sp, * rep from * to * 14 more times, 3 ch, sk [1 dc, 2 ch, 1 dc], ss in 3rd of 4 ch. 96 sts.
**Round 8:** 1 ch, [1 sc in 1-ch sp, 1 sc in next dc, 3 sc in 3-ch sp, 1 sc in next sc] 15 times, 1 sc in 1-ch sp, 1 sc in next dc, 3 sc in 3-ch sp, ss in first ch. 96 sts.
Fasten off yarn B.

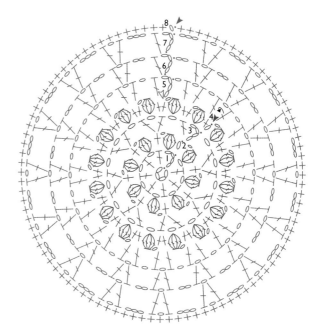

# 4
# PROJECTS

The blocks in this book can be combined and used in a myriad of ways. This chapter presents a selection of stunning designs to inspire you with ideas of how to use the blocks in your own projects.

# BUSY LIZZIE THROW

This arrangement of Busy Lizzie Hexagons (block 55, page 108) is quite simple, but by using six colors in different combinations for the blocks, the effect is rich and satisfying. A single unifying color is used for the seams and border.

**MATERIALS**

Size: Approx. 42 × 42 in (107 × 107 cm)

Aran weight wool, 50 g ball = approx. 100 yd (90 m)
• 200 g (4 balls) each of 1st color (copper), 2nd color (dark pink), 3rd color (peach)
• 150 g (3 balls) each of 4th color (powder blue), 5th color (aqua), 6th color (duck egg)
• 150 g (3 balls) 7th color (teal) for seams and edging
• Size H and G (5 and 4 mm) hooks
• Tapestry needle

**GAUGE**

Busy Lizzie Hexagon (block 55, page 108) worked using size H (5 mm) hook measures 7 in (18 cm) across from corner to corner.

**COLORS AND LAYOUT**

For each block, one of the three warm colors (copper, dark pink, or peach) is used for the central round 1, and a second warm color for rounds 2 and 3; then one of the three cool colors (powder blue, aqua, or duck egg) is used for the outer border, rounds 4 and 5. The six blocks used are numbered 1–6, and colored and arranged as per the table and diagram, right.

**TO MAKE THROW**

Using size H (5 mm) hook and following the instructions for the Busy Lizzie Hexagon (block 55, page 108), work the 45 blocks shown in the diagram, right. You will need the following number of blocks in each color combination (see table below):
7 of block 1
9 of block 2
7 of block 3
7 of block 4
8 of block 5
7 of block 6

**TO MAKE UP**

Arrange the finished blocks as shown in the diagram, right. Using size G (4 mm) hook and 7th col. (teal), join the blocks into 7 vertical lines, as shown on diagram, with single crochet seams (page 20). Then join the lines of blocks with single crochet seams in a zigzag formation. At each corner, work 1 sc into the 2-ch sps of both blocks, ss into end of previous seam, 1 sc into next pair of 2-ch sps. Darn in all yarn tails.

**BORDER**

Using size G (4 mm) hook, join 7th col. to 2-ch sp at any outer corner.
**Round 1:** 3 ch, 1 sc in same 2-ch sp, 1 sc in each sc: at inward corners, work 3 sc tog over [last 2-ch sp of one edge, side edge of previous seam, and first 2-ch sp of next edge]; at outer corners, work [1 sc, 2 ch, 1 sc] in 2-ch sp; at end of round, 1 ss in first of 3 ch.
**Round 2:** Ss into 2-ch sp, 1 sc in same ch sp, 1 sc in each sc: at inward corners, work 2 sc tog over

[sc before dec st, and sc after dec st]; at outer corners, work [1 sc, 2 ch, 1 sc] in 2-ch sp; at end of round, ss in first of 3 ch.
**Round 3:** As round 2.
Shaping on every sc round in this way makes the border slightly wavy, so the final round in reverse rope

stitch edging counteracts this effect, making the edge firmer:
**Final round:** Ss into 2-ch sp, 2 ch, work from left to right: * skip 1 sc, 1 sc in next sc, 1 ch, * rep from * to * all around, ending ss in first of 2 ch.
Fasten off. Darn in yarn tails.

*For a larger throw, repeat this section.*

| Block number | Round 1 (Yarn A) | Rounds 2 and 3 (Yarn B) | Rounds 4 and 5 (Yarn C) |
|---|---|---|---|
| 1 | 1st col. (copper) | 2nd col. (dark pink) | 4th col. (powder blue) |
| 2 | 1st col. (copper) | 3rd col. (peach) | 5th col. (aqua) |
| 3 | 3rd col. (peach) | 2nd col. (dark pink) | 6th col. (duck egg) |
| 4 | 2nd col. (dark pink) | 1st col. (copper) | 4th col. (powder blue) |
| 5 | 2nd col. (dark pink) | 3rd col. (peach) | 5th col. (aqua) |
| 6 | 3rd col. (peach) | 1st col. (copper) | 6th col. (duck egg) |

## TO MAKE A LARGER THROW

Twenty-four blocks, arranged in four lines of six, make up the repeat for the pattern. This repeat section is indicated on the diagram.

**1** Make photocopies (or tracings) of the layout shown, cut out the sections, and arrange them as follows:
Repeat the 24 blocks to make the width required, adding line 1 (or lines 1, 2, and 3) at the right, to balance the outline. In the same way, repeat the 24 blocks to make the length required, adding extra blocks in sequence at the lower edge to make the outline symmetrical.

**2** Count the number of blocks required in all. Used in the order given, for every 24 blocks you will need approximately:
1st, 2nd, and 3rd colors: 100 g
4th, 5th, and 6th colors: 75 g
7th color: 100 g
To double-check the yarn amounts required, follow the guidelines on page 29—if in doubt, it is always best to buy extra yarn.

**3** Count the number of each block (1–6) required. Work all the blocks, then join and work border as given.

# FLOWER PURSES

These charming purses are easily made from two blocks of your choice, worked in thick crochet cotton. Add a lining to make sure your coins don't escape!

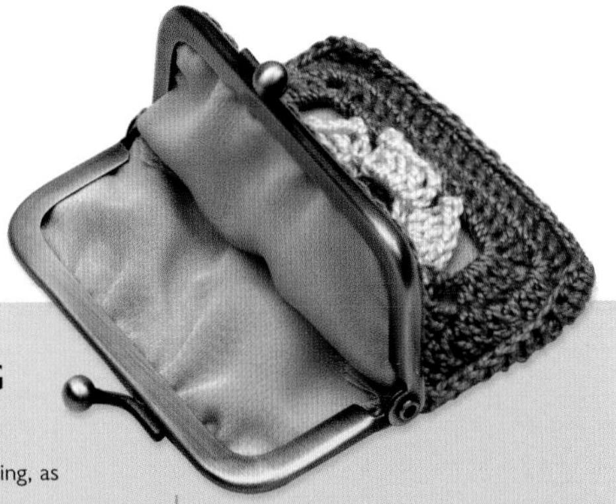

## MATERIALS

Size: Varies according to frame

Pearl cotton no. 5, 100 g ball = approx. 439 yd (400 m)
- Small amounts of cotton in colors as required
- Size B (2.25 mm) hook, or as required to obtain size
- 2½–4 in (6–10 cm) kisslock purse frame (semicircular or half-square) with pierced holes for sewing
- Tapestry needle small enough to fit through holes in frame, with eye large enough to take yarn (approx. size 24)

## ADAPTING SIZE

**To make a larger block**
- Try again with a larger hook, or add an extra round of sc to the outer edge, as follows:
- For a square, work 1 sc in each st, and [1 sc, 2 ch, 1 sc] in same place at each corner, so increasing 8 sts.
- For a circle ending with 96 sts on the last round, work [1 sc in each of 5 sts, 2 sc in next st] 16 times, so increasing to 112 sts.

**To make a smaller block**
- Try again with a smaller hook, or leave one or two outer rounds unworked.

## TO MAKE A PURSE

1 Choose a square or circular block to suit the frame. Avoid blocks with large holes. See the list of blocks used (right), to make the purses shown here.

2 Using size B (2.25 mm) hook, work one block of your choice. Test the size against the frame. The outer edge should not be stretched when sewn in place. See adapting size (below left) if you need to make your block larger or smaller.

3 When you are satisfied with the size, make another block to match. Matching the stitches, join the outer edges, on the right side of the work, with a single crochet seam (see page 20), leaving a gap to suit the frame. Darn in all the yarn tails.

4 Hold the free edge of one block in place so that the outer edge is just beneath the pierced edge of the frame, and use matching yarn to backstitch it in place through the pierced holes, spreading any fullness evenly.

5 Attach the free edge of the other block to the other side of the frame in the same way.

## ADD A LINING

To make your purse more practical, you can add a lining, as shown above.

1 Before sewing the purse to the frame, cut 2 pieces of lining fabric (lightweight silk or similar), each ¼ in (6 mm) larger all around than the block used.

2 Place these 2 pieces with wrong sides together and machine or backstitch ¼ in (6 mm) from the raw edge, leaving a gap to match the frame. Snip into the ¼ in (6 mm) seam allowance at each end of the stitching. If necessary, oversew the raw edges to prevent fraying

3 Turn the lining wrong side out, and press ¼ in (6 mm) toward you, all around the unstitched edges on both sides.

4 Slip the lining inside the purse, and use matching sewing thread to slip stitch the folded edges of the lining to the open edges of the purse, just below the outer edge.

## BLOCKS USED

**Large circular purse:** Made using the Penny Flower Circle (block 72, page 125), with green for color A, lilac for color B, ecru for color C and fuchsia for color D. The blocks were joined with fuchsia

**Large square purse:** Features the Ruffled Flower Square (block 32, page 85), using ecru for rounds 1, 3, and 4, lilac for round 2, fuchsia for rounds 5–7, and ecru for rounds 8 and 9, with an extra round of sc worked all around in fuchsia, and the joining seam in fuchsia.

**Small circular purse:** Worked from rounds 1–4 of the Coral Flower Circle (block 77, page 130), with round 1 in green, rounds 2 and 3 in yellow, and round 4 in lilac. The blocks are joined using green.

**Small square purse:** Uses rounds 1–6 of the Celtic Flower Square (block 21, page 74), with lilac for color A, ecru for color B, and green for color C. Green was used to join the blocks.

# DAISY CUSHION

This cushion is made with four Three Daisy Squares (block 19, page 72), using three different colors for the daisies. Adapt the pattern by substituting a different square block.

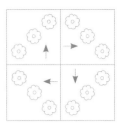

*Far left: Back of cushion*
*Left: Layout for cushion front (arrow indicates direction of working)*

## MATERIALS

Size: 16 x 16 in (40 x 40 cm), plus edging

DK or light worsted weight yarn, 50 g = approx. 125 yd (114 m)

- 100 g (2 balls) of 1st color (white)
- 250 g (5 balls) of 2nd color (wine red)
- 25 g (half a ball) each of 3rd color (scarlet) and 4th color (copper)
- Size G and E (4 and 3.5 mm) hooks
- 5 buttons approx. 1 in (25 mm) diameter
- Tapestry needle
- Cushion pad 18 x 18 in (45 x 45 cm)

## GAUGE

Three Daisy Square (block 19, page 72) worked using size G (4 mm) hook measures 6½ x 6½ in (16.5 x 16.5 cm) square (after blocking).

## TO MAKE CUSHION

### Front

Using size G (4 mm) hook, make four Three Daisy Squares (block 19, page 72) using 1st col. (white) for the background square. Work the first daisy on each square in 3rd col. (scarlet), the second daisy in 2nd col. (wine red), and the third daisy in 4th col. (copper).

For a neat result, block the squares as on page 20 before seaming them together.

Join the squares in the arrangement shown in diagram (above right), using size E (3.5 mm) hook and single crochet seams (page 20) on right side of work.

### Front border

Using size G (4 mm) hook and 1st col. (white), with right side facing join yarn at one corner.

**Round 1:** 3 ch, 1 sc in same place, * 26 sc in side edge of first square, 1 sc in seam, 1 sc in 2nd dc of next square, 1 sc in each of 25 dc, [1 sc, 2 ch, 1 sc] in last dc, * rep from * to * twice more, 53 sc along fourth edge as set, ss in first of 3 ch. 55 sc on each side. Fasten off 1st col. Join 2nd col. (wine red) in 2-ch sp.

**Round 2:** 3 ch, 1 sc in same place, * 1 sc in each sc to next corner, [1 sc, 2 ch, 1 sc] in 2-ch sp, * rep from * to * twice more, 1 sc in each sc to corner, ss in first of 3 ch. 57 sc on each side.

**Round 3:** Ss into 2-ch sp, 5 ch, 2 dc in same ch sp, * 1 dc in each sc to next corner, [2 dc, 2 ch, 2 dc] in 2-ch sp, * rep from * to * twice more, 1 dc in each sc to corner, 1 dc in first 2-ch sp, ss in 3rd of 5 ch. 61 dc on each side.

**Round 4:** Ss into 2-ch sp, 5 ch, 2 dc in same ch sp, * 1 dc in each dc to next corner, [2 dc, 2 ch, 2 dc] in 2-ch sp, * rep from * to * twice more, 1 dc in each dc to corner, 1 dc in first 2-ch sp, ss in 3rd of 5 ch. 65 dc on each side. Rep round 4 twice more. 73 dc on each side. Fasten off.

### Buttonhole panel

Cut six 10 in (25 cm) lengths of 2nd col. to use for buttonholes. Using size G (4 mm) hook and 2nd col. make 44 ch.

**Row 1:** 1 dc in 4th ch from hook, 1 dc in each ch to end. 42 sts.

**Row 2:** 3 ch, skip first dc, 1 dc in each dc, ending 1 dc in 3rd of 3 ch. Rep row 2 four more times.

**Buttonhole row:** Remove hook from working loop and join one short length to 4th dc, 3 ch, skip 4 dc, fasten off with ss in next dc. Pick up working loop onto hook, 3 ch, skip first dc, 1 dc in each of 2 dc, 1 dc in dc to which short length was joined, 2 dc tog over [same dc and into 3-ch sp], 2 dc into 3-ch sp, 2 dc tog over [same 3-ch sp and next dc], 1 dc in same dc as last insertion, 1 dc in each dc ending 1 dc in 3rd of 3 ch. Work row 2 five times in all. Rep last 6 rows four more times. 36 rows in all. Fasten off.

### Panel edging

With right side facing, use size E (3.5 mm) hook to join 2nd col. to lower corner of right side edge next to buttonholes, 1 ch, 2 sc in side edge of each row to top corner. Fasten off.

### Button panel

Work to match buttonhole panel, omitting buttonholes and working edging on left side edge.

## TO MAKE UP

Lap the buttonhole panel over the button panel by 11 sts, so making the top and bottom edges 73 sts wide, and pin or baste in place.

**Joining round:** Place the front and back with wrong sides together and use size E (3.5 mm) hook to join 2nd col. to 2-ch sp at corner of front, at right of top edge of back panels, 1 ch, 1 sc in each dc of front, together with corresponding dc of back, to overlap; at overlap, work 1 sc in each dc of front together with corresponding dc of buttonhole panel only, continue to corner; at corner, work 1 sc in 2-ch sp of front together with 1 sc into corner of back; work down side edge in same way, placing 2 sc in side edge of every row of back; work along lower edge in same way as top edge, and up second side edge in same way as first side edge, ss into first ch.

**Loopy border:** 7 ch, * 1 sc in next sc, 6 ch, * rep from * to * all around, ending ss in first of 7 ch. Fasten off.

### Optional extra daisy

Using size G (4 mm) hook and 4th col. make 6 ch, join into a ring with ss in first ch.

**Round 1:** 1 ch, 11 sc into ring, ss in first ch. 12 sts.

**Round 2:** As round 2 of daisy (page 72).

Sew at the center of the cushion.

## TO FINISH

Darn in all the yarn tails. Press according to instructions on yarn bands, omitting daisies. Sew on buttons to match buttonholes.

# ROSE SCARF

This scarf is an easy project made using the Granny Rose Triangle (block 4, page 51) worked in aran yarn. A single line of blocks will make an adult-sized scarf.

### MATERIALS

Size: approx. 8 × 60 in (20 × 152 cm)
Aran weight wool/mohair mix, 50 g = approx 153 yd (140 m)
• 150 g (3 balls) of 1st col. (peacock)
• 50 g (1 ball) each of 2nd col. B (old gold), 3rd col. (pink), and 4th col. (copper)
• Size H and I (5 and 5.5 mm) hooks
• Tapestry needle

### GAUGE

Granny Rose Triangle (block 4, page 51) worked using size I (5.5 mm) hook measures 7½ in (19 cm) on each side.

### TO MAKE SCARF

#### First block

Using size I (5.5 mm) hook, work Granny Rose Triangle (block 4, page 51), using 2nd col. for round 1, 3rd col. for rounds 2 and 3, and 1st col. for rounds 4–7.

#### Second block

Work as first block, but using 4th col. for rounds 2 and 3. Do not fasten off at end of round 7.

#### Join to previous block

Join with a single crochet seam (page 20) on right side of work as follows:
Ss into 2-ch sp, 1 ch, 1 sc inserting hook through same ch sp, and through corresponding 2-ch sp of previous block (from behind), [1 sc in each pair of corresponding sc] 25 times, 2 sc in corresponding 2-ch sps. Fasten off.

#### Third block

Work in colors as first block, joining to second block as above, to make arrangement shown in diagram 1.
Repeat second and third blocks 5 more times. 13 blocks in all.

#### BORDER

Using size H (5 mm) hook, join 1st col. to 2-ch sp at outer corner of thirteenth block:
Round 1: 6 ch, 1 sc in same 2-ch sp, * 5 ch, skip 2 sc, 1 sc in next sc, [5 ch, skip 4 sc, 1 sc in next sc] 4 times, 5 ch, skip 2 sc, ** 1 sc in 2-ch sp, 5 ch, skip [1 seam, 2-ch sp

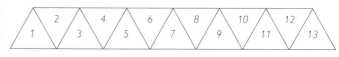

*Diagram 1*

and next seam], 1 sc in 2-ch sp, * rep from * to * to last block, work once from * to ** to outer corner, [1 sc, 5 ch, 1 sc] in 2-ch sp, work once from * to **, 1 sc in next 2-ch sp, 5 ch, skip 1 seam, 1 sc in next 2-ch sp, rep from * to * to last 2 blocks, work once from * to **, 1 sc in next 2-ch sp, 5 ch, skip 1 seam, 1 sc in next 2-ch sp, work once from * to **, ss in first of 6 ch.
Round 2: Ss into 5-ch sp, 1 ch, [2 sc, 3 ch, 3 sc] in same 5-ch sp, [3 sc, 3 ch, 3 sc] in each 5-ch sp all around, ending ss in first ch of round.
Fasten off.

#### TO FINISH

Darn in all the yarn tails neatly. Press according to instructions on yarn bands.

### TIPS

• You can choose a different block. Squares or diamonds can also be used to make a long scarf (see diagram 2).
• When choosing a block, bear in mind the appearance of the wrong side.
• The yarn weight and hook size will determine the finished size. Blocks in this book, worked in aran or bulky yarn (with a suitable hook, as page 10) will make a scarf approx. 7–9 in (18–23 cm) wide.
• For a long scarf, a good rule of thumb is to make the length approximately equal to the height of the wearer.

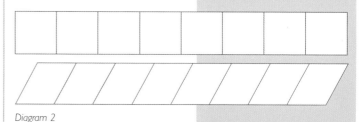

*Diagram 2*

# INDEX

## A

abbreviations 14–15
Aster Diamond 43, 98

## B

ball bands 15
block arrangements 18–19
block sizes 12–13
blocking 20
blocks 26
  fall themes 48–51
  spring themes 32–37
  summer themes 38–47
Blossom Square 36, 70
Bobble Flower Circle 41, 131
Bobble Flower Hexagon 37, 113
Bobble Square 37, 88
borders 22–23, 23–25
  block edging 24
  double shells 25
  fitting sewn-on border 23
  frilled flowers 25
  knotted loops 25
  plain ruffle 24
  small picot edging 24
Busy Lizzie Hexagon 44, 108
busy lizzie hexagon: Busy Lizzie
  Throw 134–135
Buttercup Circle 35, 128
Butterfly Circle 45, 126
Butterfly Square 40, 71

## C

care of crochet 29
Celtic Flower Circle 48, 121
Celtic Flower Square 48, 74
  Flower Purses 136–137
Celtic Flower Triangle 48, 54
Centaury Triangle 46, 56
charts 15
Chrysanthemum Square 51, 75

circles 19
  Bobble Flower Circle 41, 131
  Buttercup Circle 35, 128
  Butterfly Circle 45, 126
  Celtic Flower Circle 48, 121
  Coral Flower Circle 38, 130
  Dahlia Circle 50, 123
  Dandelion Circle 37, 129
  Floral Circle 45, 124
  Helenium Circle 48, 119
  Penny Flower Circle 44, 125
  Popcorn Flower Circle 40, 127
  Rosette Circle 36, 120
  Thistle Circle 47, 122
Clematis Diamond 38, 96
colors 27
colors: color wheel 26
Colorwork Hexagon 42, 99
complementary colors 27
construction 29
cool colors 27
Coral Flower Circle 38, 130
  Flower Purses 136–137
Coral Trellis Square 46, 69
Cornflower Hexagon 39, 101
Crocus Square 33, 77
cushion
  Daisy Cushion 138–139

## D

Daffodil Hexagon 32, 107
Dahlia Circle 50, 123
Daisy Chain Square 32, 81
Daisy Cushion 138–139
Dandelion Circle 37, 129
Dandelion Diamond 36, 93
darning in tails 17
diamonds 18
  Aster Diamond 43, 98
  Clematis Diamond 38, 96
  Dandelion Diamond 36, 93
  Four-Daisy Diamond 40, 97

Irish Diamond 48, 95
  Kingcup Diamond 34, 94
Dianthus Hexagon 47, 105
direction of working 16–17

## E

edgings 22–23, 23–25
  single crochet at inward corners
    23
  single crochet at outer corners 23
  single crochet on outer, top or
    bottom edge 22
  single crochet on side edge 22
Embossed Flower Square 41, 73
equipment 10–11

## F

Filet Flower Square 35, 92
fingerwrap 16
finishing neatly 17
flat sewn seam 21
Floral Circle 45, 124
Florette Triangle 43, 66
Flower Purses 136–137
  adapting size 136
  adding lining 136
Four-Daisy Diamond 40, 97
Frilled Flower Hexagon 42, 102
Fuchsia Square 45, 78

## G

Garland Hexagon 45, 110
gauge, testing 12
Geranium Triangle 38, 58
Granny Rose Square 43, 67
Granny Rose Triangle 44, 57
  Rose Scarf 140–141
grown-on edgings 22–23

## H

harmonious colors 27
Helenium Circle 48, 119
hexagons 18
  Bobble Flower Hexagon 37, 113
  Busy Lizzie Hexagon 44, 108
  Colorwork Hexagon 42, 99
  Cornflower Hexagon 39, 101
  Daffodil Hexagon 32, 107
  Dianthus Hexagon 47, 105
  Frilled Flower Hexagon 42, 102
  Garland Hexagon 45, 110
  Large Flower Hexagon 39, 47
  Loopy Flower Hexagon 46, 111
  Old French Hexagon 43, 103
  Open Dahlia Hexagon 51, 118
  Open Flower Hexagon 48, 114
  Snowdrop Hexagon 34, 103
  Spinning Dahlia Hexagon 48, 115
  Spiral Windflower Hexagon 41,
    106
  Spring Meadow Hexagon 33, 117
  Star Flower Hexagon 50, 112
  Swirling Hexagon 34, 116
  Wild Rose Hexagon 46, 109
hooks 10

## I

Intarsia Triangle 37, 55
Irish Diamond 48, 95
Irish Rose Square 40, 80

## J

joining blocks 20–21
Jonquil Triangle 32, 61

## K

Kingcup Diamond 34, 94

## L

Lacy Daisy Square 34, 76
Large Flower Hexagon 39, 47
laundering 15
Lily Triangle 36, 62
Loopy Flower Hexagon 46, 111

## M

Michaelmas Daisy Triangle 41, 65

## O

Off-Center Square 47, 90
Old French Hexagon 43, 103
Open Dahlia Hexagon 51, 118
Open Flower Hexagon 48, 114

## P

Penny Flower Circle 44, 125
    Flower Purses 136–137
picots
    joining with picots 21
    small picot edging 24
pins 11
planning project 26–27
    choosing arrangement 28
    choosing block 26
    choosing colors 27
    choosing yarn 26
    design tip 28
    planning construction 29
    test strips 27
Popcorn Flower Circle 40, 127
Poppy Square 50, 82
Primrose Square 33, 79
purses
    Flower Purses 136–137

## R

reading charts 15
ring of chains 17
Rose Scarf 140–141
Rosebud Square 44, 91
Rosette Circle 36, 120
rounds 16
    charts in rounds 15
    understanding rounds 16
    working in the round 16–17
rows 16
    charts in rows 15
Ruffled Flower Square 47, 85
    Flower Purses 136–137
rulers 11

## S

scarf
    Rose Scarf 140–141
scissors 11
seams 20–21
sewn-on borders 23–25
Shamrock Triangle 33, 60
single crochet seam 20
slip stitch seam 20
Sneezewort Square 50, 83
Snowdrop Hexagon 34, 103
Spanish Poppy Square 42, 84
Spinning Dahlia Hexagon 48, 115
Spiral Windflower Hexagon 41, 106
Spring Meadow Hexagon 33, 117
squares 18
    Blossom Square 36, 70
    Bobble Square 37, 88
    Butterfly Square 40, 71
    Celtic Flower Square 48, 74
    Chrysanthemum Square 51, 75
    Coral Trellis Square 46, 69
    Crocus Square 33, 77
    Daisy Chain Square 32, 81
    Embossed Flower Square 41, 73
    Filet Flower Square 35, 92

    Fuchsia Square 45, 78
    Granny Rose Square 43, 67
    Irish Rose Square 40, 80
    Lacy Daisy Square 34, 76
    Off-Center Square 47, 90
    Poppy Square 50, 82
    Primrose Square 33, 79
    Rosebud Square 44, 91
    Ruffled Flower Square 47, 85
    Sneezewort Square 50, 83
    Spanish Poppy Square 42, 84
    Star Flower Square 39, 68
    Stonecrop Square 48, 86
    Sunflower Square 51, 87
    Three Daisy Square 39, 72
    Tulip Square 35, 89
Star Flower Hexagon 50, 112
Star Flower Square 39, 68
stitch markers 11
Stonecrop Square 48, 86
Stonecrop Triangle 51, 64
Sunflower Square 51, 87
Swirling Hexagon 34, 116
symbols 14–15

## T

tape measures 11
test strips 27
Thistle Circle 47, 122
Three Daisy Square 39, 72
    Daisy Cushion 138–139
throw
    Busy Lizzie Throw 134–135
triangles 18
    Celtic Flower Triangle 48, 54
    Centaury Triangle 46, 56
    Florette Triangle 43, 66
    Geranium Triangle 38, 58
    Granny Rose Triangle 44, 57
    Intarsia Triangle 37, 55
    Jonquil Triangle 32, 61
    Lily Triangle 36, 62

    Michaelmas Daisy Triangle 41, 65
    Shamrock Triangle 33, 60
    Stonecrop Triangle 51, 64
    Violet Triangle 35, 63
    Windflower Triangle 38, 59
Tulip Square 35, 89

## V

Violet Triangle 35, 63

## W

warm colors 27
Wild Rose Hexagon 46, 109
Windflower Triangle 38, 59

## Y

yarn needles 11
yarns 12–13
    calculating yarn required 29
    choosing yarn 26

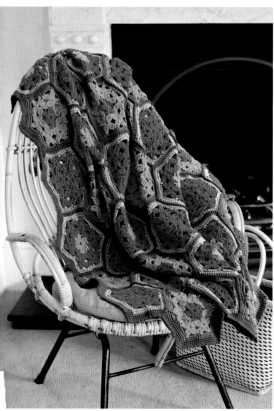

# CREDITS

The author would like to thank all the team at Quarto for their help and encouraging support.

# RESOURCES

To find local and/or mailorder stockists of materials used for the projects, visit the following websites:

Busy Lizzie throw: Debbie Bliss Cashmerino Aran     www.debbieblissonline.com

Flower purses: DMC Petra no. 5     www.dmc-usa.com

Daisy cushion: King Cole Merino Blend DK     www.kingcole.co.uk

Rose scarf: Rowan Kid Classic     www.knitrowan.com